Pause-12 months of going nowhere

Simone Mansell Broome

Based on the blog – Locklites.co.uk – written in 2020 and 2021, about life on a smallholding and rural wedding business in West Wales.

ISBN 978-1-8384580-2-7

Printed in the UK

Acknowledgements

You know who you are! Thank you.

Why?

I wrote my blog during the extraordinary circumstances of the pandemic. It helped to keep me sane and to give me a creative outlet – my poetry output had seriously dwindled in the previous few pre-Covid years. When the world started unlocking again for the second – no, third – time, I published the blog as an e-book, but with some misgivings. Almost to draw a line under the weirdness of the past year. E-books? Yes, I know – there will always be insistent, palpable magic about paper and print. I'm hooked on *real* books.

It felt, back then, in the spring of 2021, that everything was reverting slowly to 'normal'. But it didn't revert and it hasn't. Scars are still visible in public and private life. Nineteen months later, I've queued for my fourth jab. Friends and neighbours are still contracting C19 but, thankfully, cases appear to be mild. Our pandemic lexicon isn't redundant yet. And we've rolled on into a financial crisis, political turmoil and a major European war, barely pausing for breath.

So I've decided it makes sense to produce this little book, adapted from the original blog. I hope there's something in it you can connect with, find relevant or even enjoy.

Like a duck to water

Dougal, one of our two English Springer spaniels, died in April 2020, aged 14 bar a few days.

Like a duck to water

You almost didn't make it, just out of view
of the humans who sat, chatting, downing
cups of tea, amused by a clowning puddle of pups,
tussling and tumbling on new Spring grass.
You scrambled up a ramshackle pile of bricks,
stacked against a plastic butt, and somehow must
have toppled in.

Alarmed by sounds of splashing, we found you
doggie-paddling in blissful unschooled circles, ears
dipping, skimming then skirting the murky surface.
You learned fast – this first watery mishap
transformed into a story, your story –
the discovery of the aqueous element
you made your own.

Adventures in, on, across, through water
populate our memories of you. Your chest built
for swimming, ears spread wide, steady, bubbly
breathing:
your pelt liquified. Sometimes we'd panic, light failing,
scanning the horizon or bank, and no dog visible.
Would you get washed away, tire and drown
or simply carry on,

forget to turn, your easy strokes pulling you
out into the Irish Sea,
the sunset,
West?

Born to Race

This was the second of three poems I was asked to write for ITV racing, this time for the Cheltenham Gold Cup race in 2020. Technically, this was just before lockdown but Covid-19 was the reason the festival was almost cancelled. The poem which was broadcast on March 13th was a lot shorter than my original but here's one version of it anyway...

Born to race

He's not her first, won't be her last, bred
as he's been to be fast, jump, run, race.

Your heart-rate's halved and falling; it may go lower still.
Eleven moons of growing. Soon. Not long to wait. Fluid,
skin and bones, jumbled bundle of limbs with oversized head,
yet with your first breath, your stumbling steps, the stuff
of old schemes, new dreams gets made flesh.

Feed, hunker down with me, stabled, warm. Time enough
to feel long days of sun on cropped paddock extend,
stretch your legs, run just for the joy of it. They chose me;
chose your sire. A good strong start. Already. Excited,
reined-in hopes chart your progress, contrails
across a racing sky...

Is winning born or winning grown? When are the seeds
of triumph sown, for nothing is knowable until it's known?

Then the sales; sold to new owner; stable, yard; playmates,
and the slow, steady tasks of schooling. Of course it's hard,
but you're keen, bold, brave, making strong bonds
with your trainer, mastering hurdles then jumps. Race
in a 'bumper. Win. Win again, while expectations build.

Al Boum Photo, Kauto Star, Arkle,
Best Mate, Cottage Rake, and no snail - L'Escargot...

Will his name be breathed in the same breath as all those stars
since 1924, Gold Cup winners - alchemic blends of destiny,
class,
hard graft, the going on the day?

They'll talk times, assess your form. Bone over blood over
bone?
Or is it heart? You have skills, will: have known the thrill
of winning. They'll talk success - hope for more. Breaths held,
as you step out at Cheltenham. Not here as a mere hoofnote
in the jump race halls of fame. Trained and taught for now;

as the tapes lift, the race starts. Make history today!
You're not my first, won't be my last.
You were born to run. You may be my best!

Faradiddle – what a firkin!

Yesterday, mid-afternoon, the incident of note was a minor explosion. It must have been about four p.m., and I didn't actually hear it. The conservatory where I was sitting, writing lists, is across the other side of the farmyard from our little rustic bar. More of a phut than a bang then.

'Y Bar Bach' is of course not currently graced by punters, but the door to the bar also leads to our laundry area, so when I unlocked to take a pile of washing out of one of the two machines, I was met by an unmistakable smell – earthy and sweet. The floor was sticky, in parts treacly; the plug was absent and there was a slight dusting of scum on the top of the last plastic firkin of local beer delivered before lockdown. I wiped it, revealing the label – 'Amber Ale, 4.0%, duty paid on 39.35 litres.'

My immediate thought was that it was gone, wasted, useless, yet another casualty of the current chaos. And then I wondered if 39 or so litres could be poured onto the compost heap, or could I hive a little off first for some sort of smelly hair treatment? But two of the menfolk appeared and a pint glass was found to test it. 'Absolutely fine' said my son-in-law, who knows a thing or two about beer. 'But it won't keep. It'll be spoilt within twenty-four hours.' What a shame.

I needn't have concerned myself. The firkin was propped on its side on the wall by the farm gate, next to a charity pot and a packet of disinfectant wipes. One-by-one the husband, son and son-in-law, plus a few locals from the hamlet, (meticulously observing hygiene and social distancing rules), turned up with bottles, jugs, flagons and buckets. Within forty-five minutes, it was emptied.

Not everything that happens in lockdown is grim. There are occasional serendipitous plusses.

Two years on, 'Y Bar Bach' no longer exists as a bar. It's become a laundry and housekeeping room, and is where farm staff have coffee and lunch. No more dramatic ale-related incidents, just the frequent whistling of a kettle.

On grooming...

I'm thinking I'll be scruffier when this is over. Due to Covid-19, perhaps, the hairdressing salon in the village, (let's call it 'Scissors'), is closed. For ever. The cutting is not the issue. My daughter-in-law has said she'll give me a trim, sort out my fringe before it becomes a health and safety issue – I will trade with her so no problem there. But am I going grey? For ever. Will I let myself? Or will I grasp an alternative out of the bag, a hair dye bunny out of the hat? I'd have to order it online and I'd need an accomplice.

Will I embrace purple, or is that too obvious?

I'm thinking I'll be scruffier when this is over. There's a suggestion, more than a suggestion of can't- be-arsed right now. Why file my nails or pluck my brows? Who's there to see my efforts? Why bother? I shaved my legs for the first time in weeks and thought – what's the point? We're banned from beaches and pools are closed. Short, summery skirts are not practical attire for breezy, brambly smallholdings. I'll leave my lilywhite limbs unexposed. Thighs can be rediscovered another day. Or not.

I'm thinking I'll be scruffier, contentedly scruffier, when this is over.

I am. But as for contentedly...hmmm.

Cheating, scandal and milking the media

We've just been watching 'Quiz', a drama based on true events – the supposed cheating , mostly in the form of strategically placed coughs, which enabled someone, a Major Ingram, to win a million pounds in a TV quiz show Over three nights the story unfolded of the build-up to the contest appearance of Major Ingram, his win and the subsequent investigation, persecution, trial and conviction of the contestant, his wife and a co-conspirator, (a man with a tickly throat irritation).

This furore dominated the papers and TV – headlines, gossip and editorial – late in 2001 and beyond. The flames of public interest were fanned further by an ITV documentary about the scandal.

What struck me, and the husband, yesterday evening was that this story wasn't even glimpsed on our radar at the time. In September 2001 we were staying at the airport in Atlanta when the Twin Towers were hit. There was a brief lockdown and our return to the UK was delayed. In the following weeks and months we were totally focussed on trying to deal with the dramatic downturn in the fortunes of our little airline-related business. Did they do it, and does it matter were questions we didn't consider, until last night

I won't underline any parallels but here is a poem I wrote called "12th September". *It won a competition in 2007 in Winchester and appeared in my first slim volume – 'Not Exactly Getting Anywhere But...' in 2008. I entered loads of competitions in the early days of moving to Wales. From 2010 onwards, the growing family business consumed all my time and energy. Less writing; less entering; less publishing.*

12th September

And the morning after was unlike
mornings after - the world changed
utterly. And the world, or rather,

that small slice of world, the Marriott
airport hotel, was struck by
silence, by empty skies. Suddenly

there were stars, not haze or engine roar,
and we railed against blueness,
feeling caged by an infinity

which inconvenienced us, an act
of terror, like an act of
God, forcing us to juggle diaries,

put commerce on hold: and outside the
spinning doors, conspiracies
of bellboys, touts already selling

those Godblessamerica tee shirts.

No Visitors

This Easter no cars pulled up filled with hot, tired children and pooches, with couples who'd had words about directions, with tales of nose-to-tail M4 jams. This Easter there were no visitors to greet, meet, feed, water, talk to, say farewell to.

There were no visitors.

This Easter no one came to ask for an extra key, more logs, or kindling, matches or firelighters. This Easter no one needed directions, or a restaurant booking, or a taxi. There were no visitors.

This Easter there were no recommendations sought for pubs, beaches, places to walk. This Easter no one asked for the hot tub, or an extra blanket, or BBQ coals or a plaster. There were no visitors.

This Easter the children still hunted for clues, but by themselves. This Easter the only cooking smells were our cooking smells. This Easter the only noise from children was from our children.

This Easter there was still chocolate and over-indulgence; the children feasted stickily. This Easter we were favoured with fine weather and good health.

This Easter there were no visitors.

Bravery reveals itself variously

My dreams have been peopled with sideshow freaks, circus acts, feats of wild bravery, shrieks and gasps, but right now, the big top has gone and it's a grey Saturday morning. There are new sounds – distant, homogenised creature noises, and small, purposeful rustlings beside me.

Something is being constructed out of an A4 sheet of paper. Is it a plane, boat, bird – duck or swan? Is it origami practice or a rehearsal for the world napkin-folding championships, (to be held, of course, online)? I can't guess. Turns out it's a template for a little piece of lead needed to complete a window repair. This morning's project, up on scaffolding.

Sweet peas are potted on. The companionless spaniel is cajoled to walk the fields just with us, his brother gone. And another bold act unfolds, live on my phone, as a cousin's wife in the West Country shaves her head – a glorious red bob – raising money for the NHS. Heroism everywhere.

16th April – asses, loss and lemons

Yesterday marked two weeks since we lost Dougal. There is still a very large Spaniel-shaped hole in our lives but, fortunately, his brother and litter-mate seems less bewildered now.

Yesterday was also our anniversary, an oddly low-key day although, since low-key is the new normal, this shouldn't have been surprising. The twin highlights were donkey-rustling and dessert. Donkeys are cunning. Donkeys are clever. They lull you into a false sense of confidence when you occasionally relax security measures. On one such occasion, yesterday, they took themselves off to explore greener pastures and to evade capture for the day.

Now what you don't want is an over-indulged donkey grazing unchecked on lush new growth. You don't want a donkey (or two) having stomach-ache, or colic, or laminitis. You also don't want a donkey (or two) getting out into the lane and meeting traffic. At this time of lockdown however, there is almost no traffic to worry about and the two escapees seem unscathed by their adventures. They were relatively easy to catch after hours of gorging, and happy to be led home late afternoon, with no dawdling or hedgerow foraging en route.

I mentioned pudding. Having discovered a really simple vegan recipe for lemon posset back in January, the husband has made it for me many times since. Last night's pudding surpassed superlatives. Like the donkeys, we over-indulged too!

For my daughter's mother-in-law's sister

For my daughter's mother-in-law's sister
is a splendid specimen of woman, lady
of a certain age, not old enough
to be at risk, not at leisure and so,
alas, furloughed.

For my daughter's mother-in-law's sister
is fine in style and substance, efficient,
proficient in many areas. No shirker. She is
a grandmother, and she keeps a flat in Hove
with a view
of the promenade.

For my daughter's mother-in-law's sister,
deskbound for decades, now footloose, fancy-free
but for how long? She has signed an official piece
of paper. Latter-day landgirl, she must
make ready, hold steady, join willing ranks
who'll plug the labour gaps
this summer.

For my daughter's mother-in-law's sister
will be a classy fruit picker, in eyeliner,
bright blue, in cropped white linen slacks, a panama hat,
red painted toenails, practical walking sandals.
Decrees say she is needed; she must dirty her hands
for this country's good.

For my daughter's mother-in-law's sister
must go down to the fields, a trug just hung
carelessly at her elbow. No shirker,
she's a wonderful worker. She will toil

and labour and save the day
this year's harvest.

My daughter's mother-in-law's sister.

This poem was very loosely based on a story told to me by my daughter's mother-in-law. Licence has been utilised. It appeared in an anthology in 2021, 'Poems for the Year 2020' published by Shoestring Press.

Just one of 699 – Paul Hugh Derek

A cousin living in Pembrokeshire has been searching online for an obituary. No obituary is there. There may not have been one written. The death was on Tuesday 14th April in Edinburgh, one of the 699 total recorded (although we know figures, and reporting of statistics, vary) in Scotland up to 15th April.

The deceased was a widower, having married, in his middle years, a woman from the Isle of Mull. He left no children. He was half-Welsh, a quarter English and a quarter Indian. He was a former translator who worked freelance from 1979, translating from French, Spanish and Italian into English.

According to a website for the translator community – there are communities on the web for everything you could possibly imagine – Paul, the deceased, specialised in the legal, financial and mechanical engineering sectors, with expertise in reports and patents. He worked for companies and agencies including Renault, Goldman Sachs and the EEC.

He was my first cousin, another cousin, and he died of Covid-19.

I hadn't seen him for decades. The retired and retiring professional man I'm reading about is not the 19 year old who blew into and through our lives, when he had been sent on a ship from the antipodes by his exhausted mother. She had hoped my father would be able to connect with Paul, talk sense to him and 'sort him out'. Our little nuclear family admitted defeat after a year or two of trouble. According to snatches of rumour and anecdote I heard across my early years, Paul remained restless, rootless and unsettled for years until he found his vocation, his life partner, religion (again) and somewhere which felt like home.

We were in touch occasionally. The last time with any depth or meaning was a few years ago, when he flew to Western Australia to donate a kidney to his younger sister. This was not the act of the feckless chancer I recall from childhood. Paul outlived his sister.

He was my first cousin, a man of talents and contradictions, and he died of Covid-19.

A trip, a poem and a theft

I seem to cross the bridge less often these days, and of course, it's not possible at all right now. In Midsummer 2009 I drove from West Wales to Northampton in my little mini to collect a prize and to visit old friends. The prize was for the poem 'On Meeting my Cousin', in which the cousin is called Mark. The poem was inspired by the time my cousin Paul came to live with us when I was a child of five or six, just after we left Wales.

Looking back from the situation we're in where an outing to the nearest little town to visit two shops and the vets for essentials becomes a brief respite from cabin fever, this solo outing to Northampton seems like an adventurous frivolity! I must have spent more on fuel than I won in prize money. I also got horribly lost, and to cap it all, the husband's motorcycle 'tomtom' was pinched when I left the car to pay for fuel and chewing gum at a garage. Net loss then, chalked up to experience.

My last post was about Paul, who died last week. Here is the poem loosely based on the time when he was a significant figure in my childhood.

On meeting my cousin

Brown Clarks with button and bar,
grey skirt, pleated, knitted,
grey 'v' neck, bought,
red-and-grey tie, striped, far too wide,
brushed cotton blouse, white, Peter Pan,
such a daft name for a collar, my blonde hair
clipped to one side, a gap where teeth
are sure to appear soon.

This is me. And this the first time
I've met him, cousin Mark,
a barefoot man in drainpipe jeans,
marooned in a splintered glass sea,
eating a doorstep sandwich like
his first meal in weeks. This is why
they've bought bunks, why we've been told
to share. This is the first man

I've seen without a vest, smooth-skinned,
too tanned for November.
Six months we can't know about yet,
all the knocks on the door at night,
those easy promises, harder
to keep, slipping away; later,
from another continent,
the stories. This first time

he's just too foreign, too unclothed
to be family, bright
button eyes, travelling light,
trailing the unexpected.

Rainbows – yes, lanterns – no

Chinese lanterns, (released on my son's wedding day).

Look at it in a cardboard box, flown in on metal wings
from half a world away, folded on itself,
the thinnest of paper concertinas, the flimsiest of ribs:
this framework gives no hint of its promise.

This evening, we'll hold up lanterns, let them belly with air,
feel them tugging against us, let them go.
We'll have no control; they could be trapped in branches,
torn by thorns. They could be blown for miles.

Tonight we'll sack the matchmakers; you are ready
for this launching, filled with our hopes, your love.

They are more than the sum of their fragile parts;
let's watch them fly.

Back then, we did all the research that seemed required. Our
main concern was fire. We didn't want to be responsible for a
chimney or a tinder-dry meadow being set alight, or even a hay-
barn. We were assured that the paper structures would drift
gently downwards when the flame went out. And, should one
happen to snag a branch on its descent, it would just stay there
glowing until extinguished. No problem.

Our other concern was eco-friendliness – we didn't want the
carcase, the thin wire ribs to be left, littering, polluting. We
wanted it all to melt away into nothingness, leaving only the
memory of flight. So, those that we sourced had slender twiggy
struts, with not a wire in sight. We felt safe, pleased with our
sustainable alternative.

What we didn't think of, and only heard of afterwards as these things gained in popularity, was how one in flight might be mistaken for a flare, might alert one of the rescue services, might waste someone's precious time, resources.

But it took an image of an owl punctured and mutilated for us to realise that a paper bird, whatever its bones were made of, could still maim and kill.

So be uplifted; share the symbolism of airborne hopes, but just breathe your thanks and wishes into the night sky. No lighting of lanterns. We know better now.

The picture is of the tipi meadow lit up, but with wild flowers.

Don't mention the flour shortage

For a cat in lockdown it's more or less business as usual. Eating, drinking, dozing, hunting, being fussed, basking, sleeping. Repeat.

For Miss Baxter, life is pretty good. Food and water are plentiful. There is no flour shortage to furrow her brow, no compulsion to spend her days usefully, creatively or socially – facetiming, zooming and skyping. Even if she doesn't learn a new language, upcycle an old teapot, forage and pound wild garlic into pungent submission as pesto, or make the flourless cookies, (as suggested by Hugh F-W), her world will not end.

Because there are no visitors, she's less elusive than normal. She feels no need to hide away from the noise and bustle of people arriving, leaving and just being around.

Miss Baxter is unapologetic about pleasure.

Throughout the day she follows the sun around the house, finding the warmest spot to lounge, curled up or stretched out, whisker to tail-tip. Just now she's moved to the conservatory to lap up the full benefit of afternoon rays. The only sounds to disturb her are a few frantic flies, distant bleats and occasional snatches of half-conversations drifting in through the open windows, from the once-a-day exercisers, walkers, cyclists and a couple on horseback, making strenuous progress up the hill.

For a cat in lockdown in exceptional April weather, it's business, more or less, as usual, but wound down, slowed down and enjoyed with pure, sensuous, feline satisfaction.

On wit and gin

My mother worked in nursing, apart from a few brief months as a GPO telephonist, from the age of 17 to her premature death at 50. While she worked nights, I recall watching old black-and-white films with my father. Not all were age-appropriate but, if my father had been asked to justify exposing me to such material, it would have all been about the dialogue. He admired a snappy one-liner, a withering put-down. The English-only rule was broken for Raymond Chandler and a couple of those quick-fire sparring movie partnerships from the 1930s.

More modern films left my father unimpressed. He found them banal and saccharine. World-weary cynicism was one thing, but when it was combined with a laconic delivery – superb.

The first TV I remember was acquired, or rather made, by him when I was six, convalescing in bed for just under two months. Recuperating, trapped, I read a little but watched much more. Now, confined to home in the nationwide notgoingoutclub, I'm forgiving myself the dip in energy levels, the short attention span. I'm letting a lot of barely average TV wash over me, except of course for the ever-present, unavoidable news. Luckily, there's usually an evening G&T to take the edge off the relentless sadness, the vitriol of journalists, the incompetence of politicians.

And fortunately too, there's this place, and there's family.

Night skies, failure and fridges

The fridge is full, jam-packed to bursting, from the bottom two salad drawers to the top shelf, with tomatoes, and there are more puzzling things I can't even describe. For the first few seconds I'm not sure if I'm sleeping, recalling fragments of dreams or even where I actually am. This has happened a lot in the last few lockdown weeks.

The fridge in question is the small old one which works. It is totally lacking in tomatoes.

It seems like the edges of sleep, dreams and being awake have blurred a little. I'm not getting any assistance from the fancy watch I was bought for my birthday – my laziness really. I've mastered the basics of how many steps a day and how my heart-rate fluctuates, but the sleep analysis part leaves me cold, confused, with cramp in my left foot and half the duvet missing. The fancy watch, in broad terms, seems to be all about circles, completing them and then colouring them in; it beeps happily when either of these is achieved.

Apparently, my differing sleep patterns have been noticed also by the husband; I am regularly found face down planted in the bed. And this has never happened before.

Astronomically speaking, the week thus far has been an unmitigated disaster. Despite two attempts of wrapping up warm and gazing attentively and patiently up at the night sky, the results have been failure. Nothing at all. We were hoping to spot either Lyrid meteor showers or satellite trains launched by a megalomaniac billionaire. Nothing, except a spectacularly bright Venus and close observation of space-sharing cat politics – Miss Baxter and Oliver.

But in the afternoon, there was good conversation with old friends, a slowworm discovery on our walk, and an amusingly slow amble with the donkeys, gathering mouthfuls of herb Robert, of dandelions and of willow on their unhurried stableward way.

The poem below is from a very slightly more successful stargazing night – it's in 'Cardiff Bay Lunch', published by Lapwing in 2010.

Comet 109P (or no fireworks tonight)

August and they're telling us to burrow in sheds,
dust off the sunloungers, reclining chairs, maybe
just find blankets, snuggle up, look to the heavens;

not to fret if binoculars are currently
misplaced, as, though sharpening our view, these narrow
the area we can gaze at, a smaller patch

of sky. Okay, the naked eye then, anywhere,
but easier to spot in the north-east, darkest
there, waiting for meteors... in sixty minutes

we could count perhaps up to a hundred, shooting
not scuttling, their tails pointing back to Perseus,
debris shed by Swift-Tuttle. But, Last Quarter Moon,

we have a problem with your brightness, you blot out
fainter specks, mar our celestial spectacle,
dampen our hopes for blazing showers of stardust,

that brighten the night sky as they burn up in bursts
of light, of heat. Clouds too obscuring our view...plans
abandoned for the midnight picnic, skywatching

on Penbryn Beach. Back to the unlit night at home,
we sit around a firepit in the yard, see two,
fleeting streaks across the sky, Saint Lawrence
weeping somewhere else.

Sweet serendipity, a kind of medicine

It was my daughter's birthday on Thursday. Her daytime festivities comprised a walk and a picnic. In late afternoon we all came together to drink tea and squash and sing 'Happy Birthday'. All eleven of us fellow inmates gathered on what we call the terrace, but which is actually a west-facing paved area between the former slurry pit, (aka the walled garden), and a converted farm building, (now biomass boiler shed number one).

As is customary at these events, lockdown or no, there was something sweet to put the candles in. But instead of cake, my daughter had chosen to celebrate with Bakewell tart. The two Bakewell tarts made for the occasion were indeed baked well. They were things of beauty and truly delicious. Those of you familiar with the above-mentioned English delicacy will know that there is an essential jammy layer.

One of Thursday's tarts contained orange jam; the other – red jam. We naturally enquired what flavours they were. 'Fridge jam' was the reply. They had been made from surplus, from odds-and-ends of fruit, plus, naturally, sugar. And, because they were only designed for family consumption, there was no labelling – no list of allergens or ingredients. 'Lucky dip' jam was the name my mother used to give her equivalent creations. Small glass jars of serendipity, providing all of us with the perfect sticky excuse to try at least one slice from each tart.

In the previous post I mentioned a convalescence watching movies on TV with my father. Here is the poem based on my memory of those times

Medicine bears

Six weeks, two full teaspoon
of syrupy pinkness, morning, noon, night,
and my mother would dry
her hands on her skirt, perch,
silent, just till she hoped
she'd seen me swallow, then go.

And in between, there was
sleeping and waking and making
wallpaper shapes turn into bears,
hoping they'd be the gentle,
honey-bearing sort.

And every evening, Dad would come
and sit next to me, and we'd watch

old gangster films, Noggin the Nog, the Dickens
serial. *More Daddy, more.*

And he'd teach me stuff like -
twende baharini - which means, perhaps,
let's go to the sea, in Swahili.
When you're better, he'd say. *When
 you've had all that medicine,
and you're better.*

Then he'd be quiet again, and stay
till the bears went home.

Hope is the thing with...

Not feathers. Whatever Emily Dickinson wrote. I'm not a fan of feathers. Substitute leaves for feathers.

Under normal circumstances, we'd be hosting weddings right now. But circumstances aren't normal. Spring weddings have been postponed, some to later in the year and others to next year. It's not possible to predict how and when we'll be released from lockdown, what will happen with the social distancing rules, when there'll be a vaccine...

'To plant a garden is to believe in tomorrow.' Audrey Hepburn said that. To plan a wedding is also to believe in tomorrow, in the future. Leaving aside arranged marriages and dynastic couplings, a wedding is about stating in front of witnesses, whether that's just one celebrant, (as was the case here in January), or two registrars and two hundred guests, that you love each other and want a shared future.

A wedding is – stripped to its core – about saying it aloud, about intention and about hope.

There's a lot of gardening going on right now, from repotting a single houseplant to digging new vegetable beds and to larger polytunnel and greenhouse projects. A lot of this is motivated by staying in and keeping busy, enjoying fresh air and exercise, and some of this is inspired by a wish to be less dependent on the vagaries of supply, to control one's destiny one leek at a time. But however ungreenfingered you are, there's a primal human element to this too. Reconnecting with the earth, and doing something positive for the future.

One day, not too far into the future, we'll be able to hold the weddings of the couples whose plans have been put on hold. In the meantime, maybe some of them are growing things too.

A day of separate parts

A haiku is a form of poem, originally from Japan. It has three lines, with seventeen syllables, in a 5-7-5 pattern, and is meant to be read in one breath. Traditionally, haiku poetry drew from the natural world, or abstract concepts, for its subject matter and the haiku poet focussed on a brief instant in time, or sudden observation. There were other rules too, but I think that's the basic idea. A modern haiku does not necessarily keep to the form.

 I've been trying to write a haiku or two today.

> Crazed bumblebee, he
> hurls himself at glass, at last
> the open window.

> Deathwish bumblebee
> flings himself at glass;
> at last, a window.

You get my drift. Enough already about glass and windows.

One of my cousins was cremated in Scotland this morning. I've always felt, but rarely articulated it, that the end of life deserves a proper fanfare. A summing up and a sending off. These sorts of goodbye gatherings aren't possible right now. I've been trying to write a haiku or four today.

> 9.30 today
> a cremation; no mourners –
> a life extinguished.

> No funeral so
> sixty seconds of silence;
> respect for a life.

> Just sixty seconds,
> leave me these to sit silent –
> one minute, one life.

> Socially distanced
> mourning; one minute's silence –
> separate respects .

This afternoon the sky is darkening. Rain is promised and the air feels heavy. I've chatted to an old friend in Cardiff; we've done a little gardening, a little paperwork and now the arthritic spaniel is fast asleep in the office next to us. It's a day of disjointed moments, conflicting emotions...but yes, the bumblebee did escape unscathed.

The barometer drops

The barometer has dropped. It feels chilly but rain hasn't cleared the air. I was nursing a dull headache earlier in the day. Apparently, barometric pressure headache is a thing. Maybe that was the explanation.

There have been surveys, more of the 'how is Covid-19 impacting your business?' kind of thing – two completed and one shelved for another day. An email from the registrars, a furlough payroll to run – but mostly I've been holding the day at arms' length.

Before the temperature fell there were supersized bumblebees, usually more than one, in the conservatory every day, and I was getting up-close-and-personal to several – trying to rescue them. So a little bumblebee sting research over a coffee seemed apt. What did I discover? That only the females – queens and workers – sting. That a bumblebee can sting more than once. That they are less likely to sting than a hornet or a honeybee, and, most unexpectedly, that they are sensitive to colour, and particularly partial to light blue.

We've had most sorts of rain today, except the dramatic torrential sort. There's been mizzle, drizzle and steady persistent dreary rain. The donkeys, whose coats are not waterproof, have a purpose-built shelter in the field where they usually graze. We took them out late morning when the weather seemed to be brightening (and when the BBC had told us it would). They were quite Eeyoreish, biddable, a little droopy, palpably below par. A donkey does not necessarily do the sensible thing and take cover in her shelter in inclement weather. This evening, they stood soggily at the field gate, seemingly pleased to see us and disinclined to dawdle on their way home.

We passed the pink clematis which, suddenly, has fully clothed the telegraph pole in the yard. It was too damp for admiration. I'll look properly tomorrow.

On birth, rain and the time to reflect

I spoke too soon. The downpour sort of rain arrived this morning. No thunderstorm and no gloopy, sticky, tropical stuff. But still lots of it. Rain. And a strong breeze too. After weeks of unbroken stillness, the grass was freckled with pink and white apple blossom.

I did admire the clematis, but it wasn't at its best. A little bedraggled, windblown and underperforming. Rather like me today, I feel. Am sporting socks (for the first time in several warm weeks) and an oversized sweater belonging to the husband. On top of the usual ensemble.

After admiring and rinsing my two trays of sprouting seeds – (gosh, how that takes me back to the eighties and Bristol's

Gloucester Road!) – I made an easy soup. This was a riff on the spring vegetable theme, sourced from fridge finds, ranging in shades from the palest of sage to the most vibrant leprechaun green. We ate bread from a packet at lunchtime. Despite being brown and seeded, this felt very wrong. The aroma of freshly baked bread has become the new feelgood norm, rather than the exception to it, in our five weeks plus confinement.

A baby for Boris – the news popped, unbidden, onto my phone. He's joined 'the club of six' apparently. The other members, (also Members), seem to be from similarly privileged stock. Strange that. But whatever you think of Boris, what a year he's having! An eventful 2020 for him and still only April.

Also on my phone there was a video of a poetry reading. Distinctive and powerful but not the kind of material I usually read, and nothing like the stuff I write.

On Sunday, I was emailed some questions by the very keen Romanian student. One of them was the 'magic wand' one... if I were allowed to come back, be born again...those impossibly unlikely scenarios. Feeling wrong-footed and still a bit unwell, I'd now give a different answer. I would come into my creativity younger, angrier and grittier, with a lot of angst and attitude, and the ability to swear convincingly. A bit taller perhaps too; that would be good. But much grittier.

'I'm getting a bit bored with my own company,' my friend said. She's isolating alone now, as are so many others. I must remember how lucky I am.

The Romanian student at the University of Bucharest finished her dissertation and gained her M.A. Somewhere out there exists a slim volume of fifty of my shorter poems, side by side with their Romanian translations. Strange, but rather fabulous!

Epithalamium and chocolate sticks

An earlier post was inspired by the NHS lantern suggestion. This reminded me of August 2008 when, for the first and only time, on the evening of my son's wedding, Chinese lanterns were lit and released from the farm. Knowing what we now know, I naturally wouldn't do it again. Whether or not it's legal, it wouldn't feel right.

I wrote a poem for that wedding (but it was for the couple, not specifically the bride, so not really an epithalamium). However, this is such a lovely and unusual word that I've borrowed it for the title of the post.

A word that does occur in the poem is 'matchmakers'. In their human form, they've featured in the nuptial process for centuries, and they still exist in some cultures. In their confectionery form however they were invented and named some forty years before my son's wedding – in 1968. They were packaged in boxes, (with gold sheen and black lettering), made to a slide and shell design, similar to the way in which boxes of matches are constructed. They were tiny, a third of the length of the current chocolate sticks, with about seventy of them placed into each box. They were launched originally as a quality 'nibble', intended for sophisticated late 1960s adults and for special occasions, not for everyday.

What has happened in the last few weeks in my home, and in others I know about, is that the normal, the everyday and expected have all gone into a giant melting pot with the treats, the unexpected, the celebratory and the special. The future is no longer mapped out or known with any certainty, but there is pleasure and comfort in family, in friends and in the little things. And that doesn't just mean chocolate.

An infection

My sister seems to have the bug. Two cousins are also showing signs. If I were to get in touch with my sister-in-law right now, I'm pretty sure she too would be afflicted by it.

It's the family history bug, and my sister has it bad. She has moved on from the well-trodden paths, the more illustrious connections, to the lesser known and more obscure. For the first time, our mother's side of the family is being explored as well. My sister has joined family history societies and taken out subscriptions to genealogy websites. The work of delving, sifting, note-taking and cross-referencing has begun in earnest.

It's easy now to get started. So much is available online. My sister is trawling through parish registers of marriages, baptisms and deaths, obituaries in local papers, contracts, leases, legal documents of all kinds. All handwritten of course. Yes, it's easy to get started, but it requires tenacity and an eye for detail to make progress. Hundreds of clues are there to be found. Unlike a treasure hunt though, they lead not to one big horde, but to a myriad of little prizes.

In the last couple of weeks of detective work, nothing too gruesome has been uncovered. But there are unsolved mysteries. There are also so many personal tragedies: an abandoned child, children dying young, mothers dying young too, children being brought up not by parents but by other family members. Why did A leave Monmouthshire for Pembrokeshire? Why did B leave London for Leicester? We may never know. There are brief glimpses of lives abridged by disease, childbirth or war.

Red herrings swim past to distract the unwary – duplicate names in one family branch, a mistake with a second Christian name or confusion over spellings. Maybe it's simply multiple versions of the same name. Sometimes a trail, once hot, peters out into a decline in circumstances - poverty, illiteracy and just not somehow mattering enough to leave much of a written mark.

My interest is in the human stories – the past of our ancestors, recorded at a few key moments. While our present is constrained and our future is uncertain, trying to discover some of our past feels meaningful and achievable. So I too am infected with this enthusiasm.

World is crazier and more of it

Last night, when I went outside to clap – in my case, pan lid percussion – it sounded like I was clapping into silence. If there was applause down in the village, it was swallowed up by the damp air before it reached here.

Captain Tom, now promoted to Colonel, was one hundred yesterday. Amongst all the greetings, honours, cards and gifts, there was a flypast his home – a spitfire and a hurricane I think. No birthdays here, but, late morning, a large grey metal bird flew low over the farmhouse, the vegetable garden, the fields. It must have been on a training exercise of some sort, and seemed oddly out of place .

May Day's almost over. No maypole. No morris dancing. No bonfire. The lane's been even quieter today, a winter Sunday afternoon kind of stillness. We walked through the woods and wet fields this afternoon with the arthritic spaniel, the first time in three days. He had seemed too uncomfortable to take out before so we'd just let him rest, chill out. Three days is a long growing time at the moment. Grass, brambles, wild flowers, everything has put on a huge spurt. The May is only just starting to blossom. Dandelions are becoming clocks, but daisies and bluebells are co-existing happily. In the garden we have cornflowers and Canterbury bells, and all the things we don't want as well.

The news confuses and disturbs me. We all need our symbols, our emblems of hope, our Captain Toms. Perhaps tomorrow, when we eat pizza, it may feel like the beginning of summer.

Boxes – cupcakes and pizzas

Saturday May 2nd. We should have been hosting a fortieth birthday party in the Barn today – one of the many recent casualties. In the afternoon the birthday boy delivered two boxes of assorted cupcakes, four in each, for us all to share. We spoke through the open conservatory windows about how he was spending his lockdown birthday, and how he'd planned to spend it. We were touched by his lovely gesture.

The cupcake boxes were made of lightweight smooth card with a kind of rainbow band around each. We'd just been folding pizza boxes – a brief contribution to the takeaway evening – the second such event since mid-March. Making up boxes is a soothing, repetitive activity, as was also the planting of potatoes later in the afternoon.

Each potato planting pot comprised two tyres filled with earth. We put them against the fence, beyond the end of the farmyard, between the donkey stable and the double decker bus. Orla, our helper, gave each potato a name as it was placed into its ready-made hole. This was a much overdue task and a lot of the potatoes had started to look like human heads with faces and hair. Some we called 'mad scientists'. One in particular bore more than a passing resemblance to Groucho Marx.

A close friend's daughter has encouraged her to learn to knit. My friend's been following an online tutorial and can now do both plain and purl stitches. She's finding it to be relaxing, almost meditative. And of course it helps to pass the time. The multi-coloured scarf she's knitting could prove to be a record-breaker, as she's not yet learned how to cast off.

No knitting, but a little coherence

I will not be knitting my way out of lockdown blues. There will be no pots thrown nor will there be macramé potholders. No creations in crochet, embroidery, tapestry or tatting. Craft-wise I am challenged. As a child I was both very left-handed and rather clumsy. Dyspraxic might be the term used now. My mother gave up on me in frustration.

Two years after my mother died, I taught myself to knit plain squares. I was twenty-three. My first baby had a blanket made of knitted squares and a couple of little jackets...also made of knitted squares. All in red, white and blue. That was my first and last foray into knitting.

My daughter's mother-in-law is a keen and skilled knitter. My mother was too. This poem was partly about her knitting but more about her fierce loyalty, her protectiveness towards family.

Knitting

I remember the knitting, not what she knitted,
or for whom. But reading bored her
and she couldn't sit still enough,
long enough for television, thought
she was tone deaf, that music, mostly,
was wasted on her,
and though she sewed and cooked well,
took little pleasure in either,
having sister and sisters-in-law who excelled
in both. No, she knitted.

Once she sat in the corner of my room
for a fortnight, using up her leave, nurse
to my Juliet, clicking and clacking,
so that I could work
undisturbed, (some essay or other),
and so that she could bar the door
to a boy who was cruel to me,

or at least didn't love me in the way
she believed her child should be loved.
Of course, she went back home;
the essay was finished,
and I went back to him,
because, when you're nineteen,
you always know best.

Today the walk almost didn't happen, but the spaniel initiated it, leading the way and smiling. His movement was laboured, but the tail wagged. It was gain above pain. We were remembering the oak and ash saying:

Oak before ash – you're in for a splash. Ash before oak – you're in for a soak.

Oak leaves are out earlier in the hedges, but does it mean anything? Or is the delay something to do with ash die-back? It's hard to pinpoint why I feel so positive this evening. It just feels like somehow there's a little coherence through and around the chaos. Or acceptance anyway.

On the difficulties of being green

I'm not referring to the Kermit the Frog song. There was once a TV series called 'It's Not Easy Being Green',(or rather three series), set in Cornwall. It followed a family's renovations of a 400 year old farmhouse, and their 'green' journey. For a while this was compulsory viewing in our household. I suppose because we were, in a smaller way, doing something similar. But with the added challenge of trying to create a viable business. And without the film crews!

One quotation from the series was – 'I don't want to wear a hemp shirt and hairy knickers.' I have no idea if hairy knickers are, or have ever been, a thing. I can't imagine anyone wanting them. But hemp shirts – yes. Some of the nicest, comfiest, most treasured items of clothing I have bought for myself or others have been made of hemp.

Trying to be green, or as green as possible, involves making a lot of mistakes. It's not a state; it's a journey with many minor adjustments en route . And, like everything else here, it involves maintenance. Our two solar thermal systems, (for creating hot water), have been underperforming for a while. There's been no time or spare headspace for the husband,(or son who lives on the farm), to tackle the complex problems. But time became available on Saturday morning, and the solar thermal systems came to the top of the 'to do' list.

The process – which was messy and disruptive as often seems to be the case – involved hoses, ladders, running up and down the stairs in the farmhouse and much male shouting. But after a few hours, the mood was positive. 'We're on a solar roll,' said one of my menfolk.

I'd like to report that the solar thermal was indeed fixed on Saturday morning, but alas, absolute joy was fleeting. All is not quite solved yet, but, apparently, we're going in the right direction.

May the Fourth

Yesterday was Star Wars Day, celebrated by fans around the world. Apparently, some binge-watch the films, (set in a galaxy far far away), and exchange classic lines of dialogue with like-minded earthlings. 'May the Fourth be with you' is a neat little pun – an appropriate greeting for the day. I'm told it originated on May 4th 1979, when Margaret Thatcher became Prime Minister. A full- page ad was taken out in a newspaper congratulating her – 'May the Fourth be With You, Maggie!'

After the initial excitement of the first couple of films, I was unmoved by them. The youngish Harrison Ford had a certain swagger about him, but it was Carrie Fisher I admired. Despite the huge Princess Leia side bun hairdo, she seemed incandescently intelligent. I've read 'Postcards from the Edge' twice, (and seen the movie), and I felt very sad when she died suddenly in December 2016. A waste of a multi-talented individual, a woman of wit and wisdom, who had many more serious troubles to contend with than earmuffs.

The husband likes a bit of swash and buckle. He's been binge-watching, not Star Wars, but The Last Kingdom. There have been four series so far, based on a series of books by the prolific Bernard Cornwell. They are set in pre-Norman Conquest 'England' and feature kohl-rimmed eyes (the men), much horse-riding, many battles, and some unpronounceable names riddled with vowels. I've been less gripped. I have to close my eyes and ears at the gory bits. Scenes of torture, execution, etc aren't really my thing. But that period in history has always interested me, and the main character is quite easy on the eye.

What fascinates me though is the range of hairstyles amongst the male protagonists – from close-cropped to bowl cuts to flowing ringlets to undercuts and manbuns. Some beards are plaited and ornamented too. Complicated to maintain in those turbulent times I would have thought.

I am not usually trusted with anything sharp. My lack of prowess with a blade causes people to look away, hold their breaths. Over the weekend, the husband decided it was time for action. He took himself away to a quiet place and attacked his hairiness with ancient clippers, better suited to trimming the whiskers of a mouse. The outcome was not good – scalped in some places, mullet in others.

Yesterday evening he gave up his hat disguise. He traded a tidying up of the disaster zone for a bottle of wine. My daughter-in-law, who has many practical skills, came to the rescue armed with Babyliss for Men. The husband now has hair of the same length all over. It is bristly and a lot shorter than I'm used to. But he looks like he means business.

The gift

I found the head. And the spleen. And a speck of blood under my dressing-table this morning. It was my first task, after luxuriating in a very hot bath (thank you solar).

Just around dawn she'd come in through the cat-flap in the front door, up one and a half flights of stairs and into our room. She was making that 'notice me' yowl. It meant one thing and one thing only. The arrival of a gift. A live one, which she then chased around our bedroom.

In a half-awake state, it is hard to find a mouse. We couldn't see where it was, and had no idea whether it had survived or not. So we decided to catch the cat, remove her and bolt the door. There are several reasons for the bolt. This is not the time...

Cruelly expelled, Miss Baxter scratched at the carpet outside. So my second task this morning, after disposal of rodent remains, was to re-post the carpet edge under the brass strip, and to collect a small fistful of carpet fluff which had been shredded by an angry cat.

This cat is our fourth ginger and the first female. The other three went to the big feline hunting grounds far too early. Her immediate predecessor, Cooper, is buried under a juvenile walnut tree in the veggie garden. Miss Baxter is the only cat who has arrived in stages and by stealth. She was found sleeping rough in one of the barns, and she has infiltrated. Despite her appearance, she is basically just a ruffian.

It seems hard to believe that, less than two months ago, I was out of the house and into the farm office by nine every morning!

Garlic and the fairies

Going to the doctor, or the dentist, is viewed currently as a last resort. Other bugs, illnesses and health problems haven't suddenly stopped but we like to pretend they have. We're avoiding surgeries and hospitals, unless we can't avoid them.

Even the three-year-old knows about the 'nasty virus'. A couple of days ago I printed out some information sheets for very young children. 'Coronavirus' is a character in a picture story designed to explain but not to frighten. I printed out two copies for the youngest. They'll be able to colour them in as well.

I delivered a box of 'Celebrations' to their cottage earlier. Their mother isn't well so I'm not sure what we're celebrating, but the children will enjoy them anyway. Walking back to the farmhouse I picked a couple of hedge garlic leaves. And ate them. We've got chives in the grass, clusters of wild garlic by one of the yurt platforms, (sadly without its yurt right now), and hedge garlic is growing everywhere. Any passing vampire would doubtless get to the bottom of the lane, sniff the air, have a re-think and turn back. At this time of year anyway.

But the tonic fairies have visited in the night. The bottle crate is full and it's mostly populated with empty Fevertrees. Our secretive visitors may not have found a vaccine for C-19, but they could have picked up a little malaria immunity.

Last night's supper was gin-free but the garlic was flowing. A vegan mayo experiment changed, due to the addition of ramson leaves, into a runny but tasty dipping sauce for fried potatoes. Mary Tudor famously said that when she died and was opened up, 'Calais' would be written on her heart. It might be 'garlic' written on mine, but hopefully we won't find out.

I want to make a giraffe's head

The donks look awful right now. Their coats are between seasons, and they don't shed prettily. Twice a year, there's about a month when they appear unkempt and unloved.

They've rediscovered the last dandelions as a tasty snack to nibble on their way out to the field. Herb Robert and cow parsley are considered delicacies too, but fat hen is out of favour. They know what they like. Docks of course are a big no, and they avoid most wild flowers with precision. But we have to distract them,(as you would a determined toddler), from eating the oxeye daisies and the willow hedge.

Do most children still know about dandelion clocks, buttercups under the chin – 'do you like butter' and making daisy chains? I hope so.

The youngest ones' mum is feeling better, on the mend anyway. She is enthused by a new project, constructing a giraffe's head which will hang on the end wall of their cottage. For decoration.

'Like some people have reindeers on their wall,' her six-year-old explained to me helpfully. So, while we ladies were using the cottage on the back of the farmhouse as a DIY hair salon yesterday afternoon, the children were collecting oddments of chicken wire for the sculpture.

My daughter-in-law gave both me and my daughter a trim. I can now see out of my fringe and while I don't feel exactly like a new woman, I feel like less of an old one. We ate cakes again and the conversation moved from giraffes to incubating chicks to the easing of lockdown – the hows, whens and whats.

We're planning to emerge briefly from 'quarantine chic' later today and have tea in honour of VE Day. I'll bring out assorted vintage tea sets after lunch. Some of us may even put on dresses.

The season advances daily. Jasmine is opening against the wall in the farmyard, joining the clematis and the potato tree 'Glasnevin'. There's not a strong scent yet, but yesterday evening I went right up close to inhale the perfume. Sunset was staggeringly beautiful.

Paper aeroplanes and a concert (or two)

The children had made and coloured in a flag. We brought plates of food. I am surrounded by people who bake often and well, so I'd got out of the habit of baking. But yesterday afternoon I made a passable chocolate cake. The girls wore party clothes and all four kids flew paper aeroplanes in the garden. We had tea and G&Ts.

Our poor spaniel is suffering so no walk last night, or tonight. After putting the donkeys to bed and clearing up the worst of the chaos, we watched some of the VE Day coverage, including Katherine Jenkins. Now her dresses were extraordinary.

I think it was the summer of 2007 – definitely no later than that – when I went with the husband and his father to see Katherine

Jenkins live outdoors in Aberglasney Gardens. My late father-in-law had all her CDs and it was planned as a special treat for him. Because he was in a wheelchair, we were led to the front row. He had an aisle place and we sat next to him. He knew every number, from wartime classics to arias and he either hummed or sang along to all of it. People shifted in their seats and shushed disapprovingly in a very British way. We were embarrassed but my father-in-law didn't care. Or was blissfully unaware. He was having a ball.

Looking back I think – good for him! He caught shingles not long afterwards, and never fully recovered.

Today, after the First Minister's announcement, I blocked out booking calendars for another three weeks. Worries nibbled around the edges of my thoughts but I pushed them away. No visitors for a while yet. Don't know where, don't know when...

Pelargoniums and a teddy named Baby

Turns out my son had rescued it. It was on one of the sites where he and his team are building a bike track. They rescued the bedraggled teddy and put it into a digger cab as a mascot. A scruffy mascot which had seen better days. When the site was closed (due to the virus), the bear came back here with all the heavy machinery. It moved from floor to pallet to wall to floor again, too dirty and threadbare to have a small human owner.

At some point in the last week, the elderly spaniel picked up the bear and claimed it, the first toy he's been near in over ten years. 'Baby' now goes with him everywhere, sleeping, dozing, waking. Sometimes we have to take it away from his mouth in order to coax him to eat something. There is smelly comfort there and it's touching to watch. But, with or without Baby, we are very conscious that the dog is not doing well.

Today was a mostly office-bound day, the furlough payroll again, then moving accommodation bookings made before the lockdown extension to later in the summer, this winter and next spring. These may be the final adjustments, or we may need to change bookings again. No one knows.

I expected to greet today with some clarity and with a plan for the next couple of months, but I didn't. The feeling of wading through lumpy porridge persisted until late afternoon when we went out. The destination was a bench at the front of a bungalow up the lane. There a nimble 90-year-old is selling pink and white pelargoniums. I was given one of these by my daughter-in-law last week. I bought three more for the conservatory.

The wind has dropped now and it's going to be a warm evening. Spaniel is fast asleep with his Baby.

Slow-mo and speedwell.

Sleep and dreams are disturbed and strange. Energy plummeted, then has stayed low for days. I am not alone; we are not alone – in experiencing odd, conflicting symptoms and emotions. So many I know seem to have hit the lockdown wall in the last week.

A friend says – 'I almost cried yesterday. My toothbrush was taking too long to charge. I felt exhausted waiting for it: the tears were just there, ready, willing me to let go.'

And from another – 'I'm not even going to try to teach any more. I'm a parent, not a teacher. Juggling classroom, kitchen and office has pushed us to the edge. I want our relationship back. Home-school can wait.'

A third friend tells me she's given up the news for a fortnight now. TV. Radio. The ever-present phone. She's given it up. She's at saturation point. There's nothing she wants to watch or read or hear. She's full of stuff, sounds, images, information and misinformation – not sad or anxious, just overloaded.

Meanwhile witch-doctors, purveyors of webinars, gurus and influencers assault our senses. We are urged both to enjoy the slow-mo, to be kind to ourselves but at the same time to be prepared, to get in training for the cut-throat competition on the other side of all of this.

I'm not keeping a gratitude diary or forcing myself to look for any end-of-tunnel lights. When I step away, I'm cheered by a small story about the hoopoe blown off course. And by the sight of bright blue speedwell sprinkled in the hedges.

Three pet sheep and a long Latin name

On Saturday, we moved our pet sheep down from the fields by the bike park to the little paddock opposite the stable. Where they were before they had access to far too much grass. We were concerned for their health. Also, the oldest of them, Blackberry, has recurring foot issues and we wanted to be able to keep an eye on her.

Getting them down to the farmyard was an interesting operation, facilitated mostly by shaking a bucket of sheep nuts. We were also assisted by three small herders, two six-year-olds and a three- year-old. We are now re-familiarising ourselves with how vocal the sheep are.

Over the last few days, bird noise has intensified, but the air has become much clearer of ovine bleating and calling, (from the fields of neighbouring farmers and smallholders). Our three – Blackberry, Gwyneth and Gwilym – are filling the sheep noise vacuum.

The sheep paddock is also close to the new flower bed and to the tyres where we've planted seed potatoes. The potatoes, so far, are not doing very well, but I have hopes for the little shrub we planted just pre-lockdown. I've always loved any flowers, plants or trees with variegated leaves. Pittosporum tenuifolium variegatum. I don't know if it has a non-Latin name. We had one before, two houses ago, and it was an absolute corker.

There were lots of odd things about that house. It was beautiful but in the wrong place. It sat awkwardly in a garden which had had two chunks bitten out of it in the name of property development. We planted the pittosporum just after moving in. In the nine years we lived there, it flourished. It grew from a tiny plant to a huge, healthy specimen over eight or nine feet tall. I'm hopeful about this one...

Kitchen comments and weather wishes

As far as culinary success goes, the last couple of days have been mixed. There was fabulous pizza on Saturday evening – take-out again – but that was created by my son-in-law, with my daughter assisting. No, I meant personally. Me. Moi.

My new creation on Saturday was radish greens pesto. Using the leaves on the top of some polytunnel radishes and substituting sunflower seeds for nuts. Absolutely delicious.

The cornflake flapjack experiment today was not a triumph. The plan was to make something simple and sweet to be enjoyed by all ages. And not to waste anything...even if the cornflakes were slightly soggy. And gluten-free. I'd also run out of cupcake cases, so I pressed the mixture, flapjack-style, into a square cake tin. And refrigerated it. Sadly, what went into the fridge as a gooey mess came out of the fridge as a slightly colder gooey mess. No suggestion of setting.

But it's not all about looks, or even texture. We've been happily using fingers to scoop up the stickiness.

Despite the breeze, when we brought the donkeys in tonight, the air was heavy, slightly sticky. The sky was all shades of grey, even bruised grey-purple to the northwest. The right gatepost of the field had rotted away at the bottom. It must have just collapsed today. We felt extremely lucky that the donks hadn't discovered it, and gone roaming.

May, June and July are usually are our busiest wedding months. Under normal circumstances, I'd be watching the sky, comparing forecasts and silently willing the weather to hold. or to turn, by the morning of the next wedding. Despite our location – in the west, in the UK – many guests seem to hold us personally responsible for ensuring good weather for their festivities. I blame Pinterest and Instagram.

This desire not to disappoint, meteorologically speaking, weighs heavily on me for the whole season. But, tonight, what we need, what we really need, is a clearing of the air. An absolute downpour.

Earth, dust and the memory of ghosts

Earth, sand, mud – what's not to like if you're a young child? My daughter and son-in-law have just made their two children a mud kitchen for their newly created garden. There's great excitement about this. A family friend left a box on their doorstep containing pots, pans and kitchen equipment she no longer needed. So the project is completed and ready for play.

One of the donkeys likes to roll anywhere there's a loose surface – earth, sand, concrete dust. Her morning routine is two rolls in the farmyard. Down to the ground, onto her back, from there to her left side and then up onto her hooves again, with some effort. Now we have no need to keep the camping area donkey-free, the ladies have the run of the whole field. Over the last couple of weeks, Honey has made herself a grassless, dusty, shallow indentation, an earth bath, in the middle of the flat camping ground. She can now complete her ablutions there. Like Baloo the bear, she's found her perfect place to scratch.

Earth clings beneath my nails. Over the last eight weeks or so, it's become difficult to keep my hands properly clean, keyboard clean. My excuse for not wearing gardening gloves is that adult ones are just too big for me.

If there are ghosts here, we've not yet met them. Or they're extremely benign spirits, just minding their own business. We had no ghostly encounters in the last house either. But in the house before (two houses ago), where I planted that pittosporum, there were definitely presences. We all felt something.

When we left that house late in 2002, I planted, (or buried), a glass bottle and this is the poem I wrote, much later, about it.

Genie

We only ever finish a house
just as we're leaving. We move from project
to project. This one follows type – I gain
a kitchen as the boards go up – a kitchen such
as dreams are made of, magazines sold - warm
and buttery, welcoming...But spoilt by that view,

the flower bed beneath the window, filled
as it is with red-hot-pokers, forgotten toys,
weeds, all the debris of family life. We dig
it over, toil one clammy Autumn afternoon,
bury bulbs we'll not be there to see,
but find a ribbed, emerald green bottle.

I wash it, line it up with others on a cill
where light plays through. And then the dreams
begin, whisperings and murmurings, brushings
past on stairs, and calling out our names,
but the room is always empty. *We've let him out*,
my daughter says, *released him; he's like*

the genie of this house. And so, with everything
packed tight and engines running, on the move
again, we both shout *stop*, and with the only tool
to hand, a tarnished tablespoon, we dig
a glass-bottle-sized hole,
and put that genie back.

After the rains return

After the rains return

After the rains return, and children are back
in school, their days circumscribed, filled
with people, vivid with stuff;
and they've stopped playing slip-and-slide
or in the mud kitchen, or just

endlessly bouncing on trampolines, will
the arrival of eleven chicks still enthral?

New life works its magic, especially
on the young, but more so now.

After the rains return, and blue is scarred again
with the tracks of jumbos,
and birdsong and bleating is fugged
a little more by cars;
yet we can hug, go to the pub, get
our roots done, dive into buzz and bustle,
nine-to-five, the full diary, will
we thrill as business beckons?

When 'new normal' is bagged and boxed
for the bin men, will we shrug it off,
slip back?

After the rains return, and news is
other than this plague, will
we submit to gaining our liberty,
while losing our balance? When we stop
waiting for the when and how, stop
clapping, will we chat and gossip
at the gates,

but waste less,
less life,
less time,
after the rains return?

A welly and a gift

The second May Bank Holiday weekend. Like the first, but gustier. The guys did pizza take-out again on Saturday, minus the awning. Wind caught and tore it during Thursday night. A clean rip about a metre long. We're awaiting tape to arrive in the post so we can repair it.

Wind is the main enemy of a venue with any level of dependence on canvas – whether for food-service, wedding receptions, shelter, accommodation or all four. We've had a few issues with wind damage in the past, notably at the beginning of last season, with the triple tipi. Replaced within days of course, no thanks to the insurance company...

I've been thinking about the May weddings held here when we first started. There was no pagoda, so no possibility of an outside ceremony. Weddings then were all conducted in the Old Dairy and thus tended to be a little smaller than they later became. One May wedding I remember very clearly, partly because the photographer gave us a duplicate album for us to show to prospective couples when they visit us. The couple were lovely people and, in the almost two-year-run-up to their wedding, we got to know them quite well. The husband (mine) was in awe of the bride's rich Swansea accent.

Welly boots were everywhere for that wedding. Little ceramic ones in all the colours of the rainbow and more. Some were filled with flowers, others just placed randomly about the farm.

A few days ago I found the last surviving welly, a green one, tucked into a wall niche outside Ceridwen, our self-catering house. Finding the boot brought back lots of memories, including one of an unexpected arrival a couple of weeks after that wedding, a substantial slate disc with our logo carved into it. The bride's father had made it for us. I see it outside the farmhouse every day and am still touched.

> Father of the bride
> brings a gift: it marks the part
> we played in *her* day.

What's in a name?

Sister Rosalie -(must have been Mary Rosalie but we missed out the Holy Virgin)- used to take us on a nature walk at least once a week in the Summer Term, but regularly throughout the year whenever the weather permitted. We always followed the same route, wore our hats and walked two-by-two. It was a real treat. Afterwards we emptied the trove of finds onto the nature table, where it was arranged, identified and labelled. Sometimes we'd do leaf rubbings with wax crayons while the lovely sister read to us.

Between then and now, I've forgotten many of the names of trees, wild flowers and all the finds I was so familiar with as a young child. So it was a real pleasure when we had a foraging walk and workshop here last year. We love hosting workshops here, whether for a couple of hours, a whole day or a few days. They don't make us much money, but it is a joy to witness the pleasure they bring to people! By providing the venue and the refreshments, we are sharing, in some small way, the enjoyment felt by the students.

One of the plants we identified with the foraging tutor was very small, bright green, growing in dusty cracks in the yard and on paths. You could easily miss it. Apparently, it can be used to make a pleasant tea. It's growing everywhere right now. For such an inconspicuous plant it packs an aromatic punch. The name is pretty good too!

> Pineapple mayweed,
> pinch between fingers; release
> the scent which names you.

> Low unshowy plant,
> an explosion of sweet scent,
> pineapple mayweed.

Too hot to trot, or the blackbirds bathe

I've put two eco pond-clean sachets in the trough in the conservatory wall. Sadly, all is still green, gloom and murk. Not in any way fish-ready. Hoping for a miracle I checked again earlier and disturbed Mr and Mrs Blackbird, who were cooling off and enjoying their private ablutions. I'm not sure who was more startled.

The husband is walking the boundaries with someone who may be renting three fields to graze her horses on. It's been over six months since the last ones moved away.

He called to the old spaniel, who was dozing on the quarry tiled kitchen floor, to see if he too would like to inspect the hedges. Enthusiasm – zero. It reminded me of a poem I wrote in a May when we had both spaniels, and they were young and full of energy. But still capable, very occasionally, of being underwhelmed and lacking in enthusiasm. That poem, 'Against the grain' was read on Radio 4 in an Ulster accent – surprising to me, but effective. The only time I've had one of my poems chosen to be included on 'Poetry Please' and a great honour.

Update. We will soon have three new four-legged guests. Their owner pronounced their new residence to be 'lovely fields'. But we knew that already.

Against the grain

Early evening, May, the sloping field –
we call it that but they all do –
slope - the grass long, lush, wet, as yet ungrazed
by the neighbour's cows, the sun low,
hawthorn blossom and buttercups, and the one thing

needed to complete the picture is your dogs,
spaniels in stereo, crop circling,
patterning the meadow for the hell of it.

Tonight one dog's lazy, doesn't bother
to run the perimeter, to kite the rectangle,
to rootle and pounce, he can't be arsed.
If he were two legged this would be
a duvet day, he'd, just now, have been bullied
into stretching his legs, clearing his head,
getting some fresh air before that first glass
of wine. Tail at half mast, poor attempt

at a wag, he spots his brother
having a good time, being as loopy as they're
meant to be, chasing phantoms, that four
legged bounce of prairie and savannah,
He drops his boredom like a spent match,
races off, white tail a rudder through the green,
ducking and diving, catching up, carving loops,
contrails of clock grey clouds following following.

Aunt Jane

My cousin Paul died of C-19 a month ago. His mother, Ruby Valerie Jane, my father's older sister, was a favourite of mine. She was intelligent, rebellious, a successful businesswoman and more than a little mysterious. In later life, she painted, researched her mother's family tree and was, I'm told, a Scrabble champion.

In her youth she was beautiful, an exotic flower blooming in West Wales. There are conflicting family stories about her private life. I wrote this a while ago and found it recently. Some of it may be true. Or very nearly.

Guests at a wedding on a chilly March day, he stands behind
her, leaning ever so slightly over her, head and shoulders and
half a chest taller – a long, dark, solemn man with a lean-jawed
face gazing at the photographer in the distance. No smile on his
face but a hand, broad and bony, is resting on her shoulder, the
spread of his fingers claiming all and more of the space
between the edge of the velvet collar and the seam at the top of
her sleeve. Mine, he says, and aren't I the lucky one? The coat is
fitted neatly to an obviously neat waist, fastened by a single
oversized button. Dark shoes with rounded toes, their platform
heels just visible. Gloved hands clutching the handle of a small
bag: a hat set at a jaunty angle, perched on formal and
elaborate curls. And her eyes are looking at nothing. Even from
the distance of over half a century, they're shiny, dark and
unfathomable.

I know now that she married him soon after, that they
emigrated with her three almond-eyed children. Back home,
he, her second husband, was seldom mentioned. She moved to
Auckland, then back to Australia, was mentioned – the grown-
ups whispered – in some scandal, and moved on again, this
time shedding each child in a different establishment –
boarding school, art college, university – in different countries
across the southern hemisphere.

When she returned, briefly, to the country of her birth, she had
miraculously acquired money and respectability, along with an
ampler girth and a lavender-coloured chignon. This was when I
came to know and love her. Aunt Jane's conversation oozed
humour and a certain worldly, pragmatic wisdom. She was a
small, powerful woman who was not to be trifled with!

Devious cunning or a rare rant

Sometimes I am appalled by cats. So much carnage. Such cruelty.

It must have been a 3-kill morning. There are neat piles of indeterminate innards across the conservatory floor. Now of course, she, the culprit, is stretched out on a sofa, not a whisker out of place, catching the late best of the sun's rays. Cats have no conscience or moral compass, but equally no subterfuge, no-self-justification, no bending of the rules, as she has none. She is what she is – a killing machine, but she's our killing machine.

Dreams of trips to Durham and conspiracy theories. I spent a lot of time online yesterday, reading articles and signing a petition or two. The man has to go. I hope he will.

The first thought in my head this morning was that DC's name, as well as that of Emily Maitlis, (and mine too), all have five syllables. Each one could form either the first or last line of a haiku.

> Well done, Emily!
> He's made those who struggled to
> keep the rules, feel fools.

> Emily triumphs.
> 'Deep national disquiet'
> speaks for all of us.

> Emily Maitlis
> says it as it is. He takes
> the country for fools.

Savage brilliance
from Emily. 'Idiots' –
that's what the man thinks.

And an attempt at a tanka – why is a five line poem so much
harder to write than one with three or six lines?

Gaslighting, I'm told,
is what politicians do,
changing black to white,
making false true, tales of pride,
a long car ride...no-one's fooled.

Friendship, flowers and heroism

It was the birthday of a very good friend of mine last week. We have decades of shared history and shared memories, children, dogs, holidays and celebrations. We have favourite books in common, and lines from books we both treasure – characters and quotes acting as shorthand for our friendship. Ordinary stuff and special stuff.

In many ways we're very different – my friend is a practical soul, skilled at her craft, a DIYer, a knowledgeable gardener. She's visited the Chelsea flower show many times as it falls around her birthday. Not this year though.

In terms of the non-earthly elements – water and air – she is also far braver than I am. She, and her characteristic common sense and helpfulness, featured in a few of my earlier poems.

May 21st, my friend's birthday, was also the anniversary of the first solo crossing of the Atlantic in 1927 by plane by Charles Lindbergh. New York City to Paris. Non-stop. His flight was in response to a challenge set by a French-born New York hotel owner, Raymond Orteig. He offered 25,000 US dollars to the first successful aviator. Lindbergh followed six aviators who had died in their attempt to make the crossing. His flight in 'The Spirit of St Louis' from Roosevelt Airfield, Long Island to Le Bourget Aerodrome, Paris took 33 hours and 29 minutes. Lindbergh was twenty-five. He became a national hero and an international celebrity.

Agatha Christie based her story 1934 story 'Murder on the Orient Express' on the mysterious kidnap and murder of baby Charles Lindbergh, Jr two years before. In Christie's tale, the sex of the unfortunate toddler is changed. Her name in the book is Daisy Armstrong.

Burgh Island in South Devon was a favourite bolthole and writing retreat for Christie. It is also the setting for two of her novels – 'And then there were none' and 'Evil under the sun'. The main building on the island is a fantastic Art Deco hotel which we visited (the husband and I) the day after a Devon wedding in 2011. A trip to the Burgh Island Hotel was a long-held ambition, and the visit and lunch there did not disappoint.

In its blurb the hotel states that it's been 'welcoming famous and infamous guests since 1929'. Having been there once for a few hours, and soaked up a little of the very stylish, period ambience, the new ambition, for this neither famous nor infamous woman, is to stay there. Just once. Unlikely, but who knows?

From the delights of Art Deco, back down to earth with a bump. This is what's happening regularly now with the spaniel. He's falling. He can't manage the steps between conservatory and kitchen. We've put up a ramp. It's not helping.

Surely time for shearing

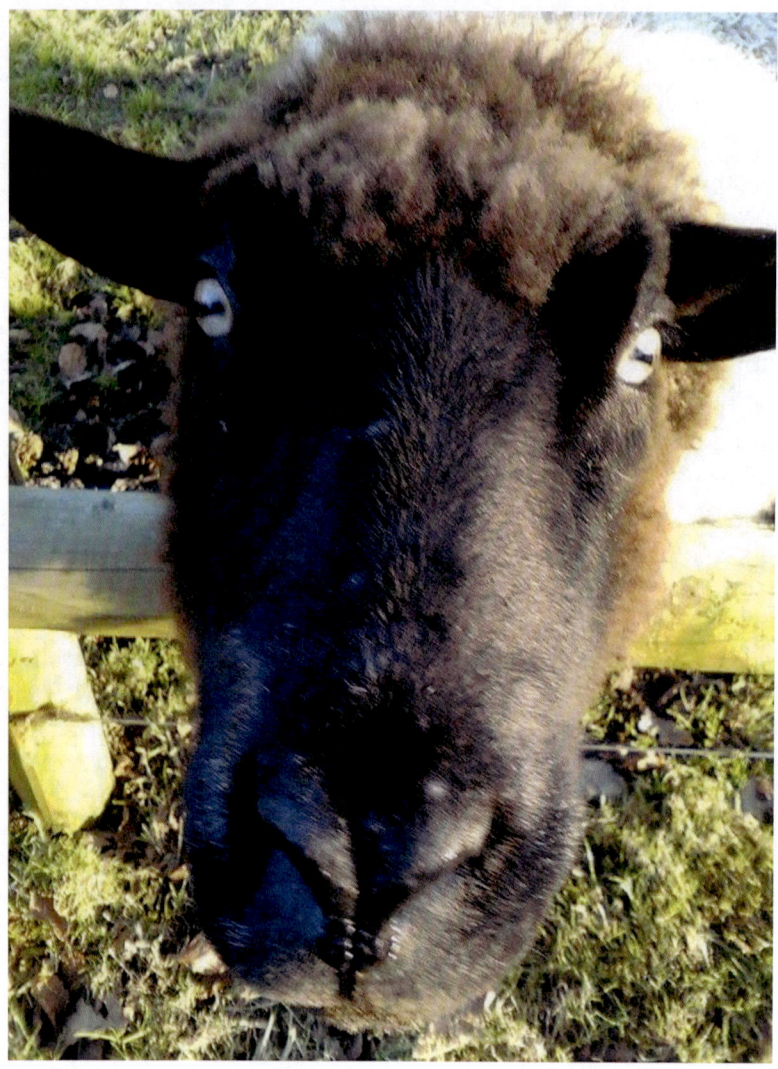

The sheep need a haircut. We've got three. They're pets. The eldest, Blackberry, is a bit scraggy and scruffy now, quite frail with regular foot problems. She still likes being petted, enjoys eating, shouting and she is indisputably the boss.

The highlight of their day is sheep nut time, early evening. Sheep nuts must be absolutely delicious, but, sadly, slugs like them too. Some huge slithery specimens have made it into the dustbin where the nuts are stored and have gorged themselves. We've swapped bins today for a newer one with a snug fitting lid. It might keep them out for a while but I'm not holding my breath. What we really need is hedgehogs!

Our first sheep was Dave. My sister, who lives in Buckinghamshire, was given two orphan lambs to bottle feed. Mildred didn't survive, however her brother thrived and became friendly and inquisitive. He soon outgrew my sister's garden. When the farmer next door offered to take him back so that he could fulfil his ovine destiny, my sister and family baulked at the thought of Dave as lamb chops.

So, he came to us. Or rather, the husband collected him. A round trip of 416.4 miles. 208.2 miles of it were spent with Dave bleating on the back seat of the old Landrover, and in the driver's left ear. Dave, not Dai or Dewi or Dafydd, was a noisy and nosy individual, who charmed both us and our visitors. Although, we hadn't planned to have a pet sheep, when he died there was a woolly gap which had to be plugged quickly.

We're waiting to hear back from the shearer, hoping he can fit them in soon. It must be unbearable under all that wool.

Red kites and Blue Peter

I've been watching a red kite circling this afternoon. I can't see it now but it's not far away. There's that distinctive cry. Back in 2012, when my sister was bottle-rearing the twin lambs, if she saw kites, she would, just to be safe, put Dave and Mildred into the guinea pig run.

We should be getting ready now for our dog show and family fun day. Last year was the first year and it was a huge success. A good turnout, great weather and everyone seemed to enjoy themselves. It felt very much like the summer fetes of my childhood. But with no rain.

Today is the third anniversary of the death of John Noakes. Watching Blue Peter, and receiving the latest Blue Peter annual as a gift every year, are clear childhood memories.

Not getting my autograph book signed by John Noakes

I never had a Blue Peter badge,
not one. I wasn't a joiner,
a taker- part. And as for Brownies,
though the plan was always to get
a raft of badges to buck up
the drab, ditch-water brown dress,
I didn't. The pony-trekking trip
was also , it must be said, a flop.

Instead I sang, recited, read,
my head full of dreams and stories.

There was a fete once, some wet Berkshire
village green, Bradfield, Burghfield
or wherever, and he was there
with his dog. Was it Patch? What a thrill.

He was there as judge of pets,
art, fancy dress, cakes or carrots.
Or all of them. You know the drill.
And it poured. Relentless.

We sheltered, he and I, under
damp canvas, watching the drips
at the scout tent door, drinking
sweet weak tea, just willing it all
to end. Did I get the autograph?
No. But I stroked the dog instead.

Much to applaud

It was the last scheduled clap last night. There's been little audible round here, but it's hard to hear above the birdsong and we don't have immediate neighbours beyond the tribe. Eight is also a bit late for the smalls. Still, they have painted a sheet with a cheery rainbow message, and it's suspended from trees facing onto the lane. And there is more to appreciation than applause.

Today began with escaping donkeys. One of the cross-rails of their stable enclosure had broken, they'd limboed under it and were off. Happily alternating between chomping on grass quietly, and then, kicking up their heels in joyous come-and-get-me-if-you-can friskiness. They weren't free-range for long. The lure of two buckets of donkey nuts proved too great. The bar's now fixed.

Another successful fix is WATER. Late morning the water pressure dropped. We were all planting in the meadow above the polytunnels. We'd sown seed and grown a vast number of wildflower plants. It was time, past time really, to transplant them to the field. But the ground was hard and bone dry. We were all wilting in the heat. And then the water stopped. The three year old diagnosed the problem as a 'kink' (his favourite word this morning) in the hose. Alas, this proved not to be so.

We aborted today's attempt at meadow prettifying. Miraculously, around 4.30 this afternoon, the water was back on. The explanation? A pump 64 metres down in our bore hole had tripped. Apparently, it's the sunniest spring since records began in 1928. And although we've still got two days left, it could well be the driest May for 124 years. There are murmurings and warnings about drought…

Stardom, Elvis and a dream

Another May wedding which still stands out for me was in 2012. We've not had many with themes, but this was a rock 'n roll wedding. The evening's entertainment was a pocket Elvis, from Malta, via Coventry. This poem, which has changed over the years, was inspired by that wedding.

E. P., an encounter.

Darkness over these ripe Welsh meadows,
las vegas, fretted
by strings of fairy lights, solar, blue,
along May hedges, elder-greening,
blossom-bursting,

by cigarette glow, (a rogue few),
by crackle and hiss of logs from the firepit –
where folks huddle warmed by blankets,
chat, whisky.

Well met by moonlight, proud incarnation,
thrusting the King's torch, rocking 'n rolling,
owning that suit, spritelike guest
at this night's nuptials, starblest,
incandescent, lighting up
the loin-lost gaze of his admirers,

who have seen a vision, divine
and otherworldly, (in fact from Malta),
shimmying gifts – lyric, liquidity
of hip, of lip, filling full his
luminous leathers.

Now, far from home, awaiting his team,
he shivers in built-up shoes –
I AM NOT COLD; I HAVE PERFORMED.

Elvis takes his leave, cash, applause,
his black truck back,
not loving us tender yet still shaking
some chill, silvery spell,
as tail-lights reveal
sequins shed on bluebell, cow parsley
and nettle at the field gate,
our lane pitted with stardust.

This was earlier in a May that was sunny and warm, but not record-breaking. The bluebells have almost gone now, and the tall nettles are to be avoided. Rather than being new and just there as a reminder of my rather haphazard foraging. Cow parsley miraculously renews itself every night, (after being consumed voraciously the day before). Jasmine still intoxicates, but clematis has been replaced by dog and climbing roses. Hot reds and foxgloves are popping up, and lavender is a few days away.

In dreams last night I was saying goodbye to a friend who was off on a space voyage a few days later...as a tourist. Not as a solo passenger, but I think there were to be just six of them. My adventurous friend and I were drinking tea and eating cheesecake outside. Wherever we were, the spectre of C-19 still lurked behind the arras. There was talk of 'social distancing'.

I think I'll set myself the task of making a list of all the words and phrases I didn't know, or need, or use, pre-lockdown. I'd like, if it's possible, to ban them from my post C-19 vocabulary. *Sadly, this hasn't yet occurred.*

Lady Lindy : why does he call you Eeyore?

Previously, I mentioned Charles Lindbergh. No-one tried to repeat his solo transatlantic crossing for five years. And then, the someone who did attempt it in 1932, was a woman – Amelia Earhart. Just as Lindbergh had done, she set off on May 20th. In bad weather she was blown off-course but she did make it to Ireland. Not to Paris, but still across the Atlantic.

What I didn't realise is that she was selected for the role. There were other potential female candidates, but she had the right look, the right image. She even resembled Charles Lindbergh, and the media often referred to her as 'Lady Lindy'.

There are two monuments in South Carmarthenshire to Earhart. These mark her crossing in 1928 as a passenger, (and keeper of the flight log), in a seaplane called 'Friendship'. The records in 1928 were for the first female crossing of the Atlantic, not solo and not as pilot. There's some controversy about the landing place. When this is over, I'm going to visit both Pwll and Burry Port, the two contenders.

The wearing of two hats, or more, is common in this part of the UK. It's necessary for survival, for making a living, to be versatile and multi-facetted. We have many strings to our proverbial bows. To an extent, this place attracts diversity and eclecticism.

The lady who works at most of our weddings as our bar manager, is a very talented ceramic artist. Her friend is a sculptor and a teller of jokes.

I know how they work, with the pay-off and punchline. Some can remember and deliver jokes with aplomb. I can't. Or I've never really tried. Pretty sure it wouldn't be my forte anyway.

Apple decided it knew better when I tried to send the husband a text the other morning. I was in still in bed, answering emails and messages, and writing a haiku. It was about 8.30 and he was already in the barn, doing some useful DIY. I was trying to ask 'have you fed the Eeyores?' but predictive text insisted I was enquiring 'have you fed the retirees?' *You know – the ones we keep locked in the barn...*

Later, after I had explained this example of smartphone interference, my listener started on one of those man-and-mate-went-into-pub stories. The landlord – to clip short a rather unruly shaggy dog – asked, 'why does he call you Eeyore?'

Man at the bar replied, ' I dunno...'ee yoreways calls me that.'

It's how you tell them really. You needed to be there.

But isn't it strange how alien a man-going-into-pub anecdote sounds after all this time?

Flaming June

The first day of Summer, though it feels so familiar. And there have been flames, a grassland and forest fire a couple of miles away, which started late yesterday. Driving to buy some garden plants this afternoon, from a small local nursery with an honesty box, we saw plumes of smoke. And a flash, as sunlight caught the moment a helicopter tipped its cache of water on the blaze. It's just so dry. We came past scorched lawns and banks – very unlike West Wales.

It would have been my mother-in-law's birthday today, an indomitable little Yorkshire woman. Tough exterior but a soft centre. I still miss her. In a rare moment of abandon, she slipped off her chair at my sister's wedding. She blamed the upholstery rather than the bubbly.

Today is also my sister's wedding anniversary, her 29th. She's messaged me a picture of the table set before the celebration tea-party. Fizz, flutes, cakes, china and a tablecloth – very English country garden. The wedding was like that too – a small affair for about forty or so people. A Victorian church, top hats and tails for the key males. The bridesmaid wore Laura Ashley. There was much sunshine and it was all quite lovely. More charming and more understated than the traditional weddings of 'Four Weddings and a Funeral' three years later.

It's been a day or two of projects. My son has hung cargo netting – donated by a friend – between trees in the veggie garden, for the older ones to play on. It's in an area of dappled light, not the full glare. Just what these fair-skinned girls need.

The husband has been making taps – copper ones – out of odds and ends, leftovers and gifted pieces. They've been drying outside in the sun post their anti-rust coat of oil. My one-and-only washing up bowl was deployed in the cooling process after soldering yesterday. I'd only just retrieved it, after it had been borrowed on Saturday as a temporary home for goldfish. They've been moved now from small pond to bigger pond. The eco pond clean solution has still not worked, so it was hard to find them this morning. But we did. All four.

This evening the new equine guests are moving onto our fields. I'll visit them tomorrow.

Sunstroke and water

Around 200 hectares of damaged grassland and forest. The last time I checked the local news online, the fire was still burning. A hectare is just under two and a half acres, so this is insignificant set against Australia or Indonesia. But's still horrible and it will have caused, and be causing, enormous harm to our wildlife.

Nellie has sunstroke and has to be kept in to recuperate. Her owner popped down the lane for a couple of bales of hay for her this morning. She and her mother, Bonnie, are Welsh cob x Shire horses. For the last few years, they've pulled our cart for the wedding couples who've opted for this mode of transport.

Investigation of the on-and-off water situation was ongoing today. The current thought is that the level is low but not critical. A pipe leak was found and repaired. So far so good.

The sheep have barely stirred today, except of course for their evening nuts.

They've been immobile, hugging the shady edges of their paddock. Two days to shearing. I want to tell them – not long to wait – but they wouldn't understand. I've had to cancel the spaniel's coiffure appointment for later in June. Trisha, the lovely mobile dog groomer, has been allowed to resume her work, but with very strict guidelines. I've decided this new regime would be too traumatic for our old spaniel, so he's going to stay unkempt.

On the phone to my sister this afternoon, we riffed on the endlessly entertaining topic of the state of our roots, and what we may or may not be doing about them anytime soon. Despite being more unlocked there, over the bridge, than we are here…there is still no salon excursion on the cards for her. Neither of us will be going purple. Jenny Joseph's 'Warning' was written in 1961 when she was only 29. Its purple referred to clothes, not hair. In 1996, There was a BBC poll for the most popular post-war poem and 'Warning' won, beating Dylan Thomas' 'Do not go gentle into that good night'. Jenny Joseph's poem, (however dated some of the references seem today), has been a notable ode to nonconformity, especially female nonconformity, for almost sixty years.

We had a few wedding enquiries today, one from a woman who should have got married in Barcelona two days ago…so many personal disappointments and thwarted plans over the last ten weeks or so. I've been recalling the only two non-UK weddings I've been to – one in Northern Spain and one in Croatia. Both sunny and warm as you'd expect, but there was a fierce thunderstorm during the Croatian reception.

Rain, rain, rain. We've been promised a drop in temperature and light showers tomorrow. Fauna and flora – everything needs it.

What sort of urinals should we have

The temperature's dropped. We've had some trifling, inconsequential rain – nothing that seems like it means business. The atmosphere's still and heavy. Typically, for Saturday afternoon and evening, when my son-in-law will again be cooking wood-fired pizzas, more serious rain, and wind, is promised. The canopy will need to be repaired by then.

There's been talk of how to set up the shearing tomorrow. What happens re social distancing? What if it rains?

The four fish have survived their house move, and, since nature abhors a vacuum, the kids have conjured up a toad. As a new resident for the former pond. I'm not yet sure if this is a real amphibian or a product of their imaginations.

I couldn't sleep last night. My brain was racing. So many conflicting views of what's actually the right way forward now; so much information but who to trust? So much feeling of impotence about the current US situation. And there, in the middle of the night, the quiet awareness that our spaniel is slowly fading. I drank a glass of water – (yes, it works!) – sat in the kitchen with the dog and let it all wash over me.

Earlier yesterday evening, after checking emails and posting my blog, I returned to the farmhouse kitchen. 'Good,' he said. 'You're back. What sort of urinals should we get?'

This is not my area of expertise, so that line of conversation was not going anywhere. But I listened, and I did learn a little. He's made his choice, but along the route to a decision, it struck me what a balancing act design and construction is, with different costs, financial and environmental, for each option. A minefield, or a reed bed, of possibilities.

And so the project moves on.

A June day sampler

A fourth horse has moved in. We went to visit them this morning and all seem happy with their new quarters. The foal is as delightful as all baby animals are.

Waiting for the shearer yesterday, organizing the sheep and then getting them back to the right field – it seemed to take up most of the afternoon. One of the donkeys, Honey, put her head over the fence and seemed amused by ovine antics. Especially those of the big boy, Gwilym, who was less than 100% engaged with the process. I'm hoping we find a use for three fleeces. It's such a waste otherwise.

There's slow, steady progress on the loo block in the first shipping container. This is turning out to be a huge undertaking, far more so than anticipated. Only the husband, and the one guy who lives on the farm with us, are working on it. Everyone else is furloughed or, in one case, abroad.

Next year, (how hard it is to imagine 2021 operations), guests using the Pole Barn won't have to use portaloos or wander down the yard to use those at the Dairy. This project follows the usual pattern. We repurpose or upcycle as much as possible. We buy what materials we can locally, and then the rest arrives via Parcelforce, or Hermes, or any of the national carriers. Deliveries are slower than before.

The weather's changed over the last few days. It's cooler, cloudier and windier. Petals and blossom have been shed in the breeze, so the whole effect is wayward and unruly now. Not that anything was manicured before – far from it.

I've heard news that my niece's zoom interview went well this morning, and that she has a second one next week – good news from over the border!

But here a single magpie almost flew into the office. I've inherited the superstitions of my female forebears, so I'll need to find a second magpie soon...

Gather ye roses

Alfreda Claire Mansell (nee Whitlock). Today is the anniversary
of my mother's death. She died in unusual circumstances,
suddenly and far too early. It doesn't really get easier with time.
I feel sad every June 5th about the years she missed and the
time I've spent not knowing her. There are no photos of my
mother at my wedding and there are no photos of her holding a
grandchild. She left us as my sister and I were on the cusp of
adulthood.

She thought they were both naughty boys

She thought they were both naughty boys
and smiled. If knicker-throwing had been part
of her experience, I wasn't told.

Frank Sinatra, Tom Jones – her heroes. For my mother
it was neither lyric nor melody. She felt
she could not sing, she knew

she could not play. It was spectacle, sex appeal,
razzle dazzle, big budget musicals, colour
and sequins, stardust

and the London Palladium. And as for the women,
Streisand and Bassey – big voices, big frocks,
big personalities, attitude,

fighters and survivors, neither prissy
nor pretty...often you'd catch her humming
over the vacuum

or the twin tub, when she thought herself unheard,
and she'd be serenading the big spender,
or remembering how she'd danced all night.

Sourdough and sad tales

It was a quiet weekend, cool, grey and yes, we had rain. The real wet stuff. Which makes the lowering of water level in the new pond all the more surprising. The pond-clean sachets have finally worked. The water has cleared from the grime and slime of a week or two ago. There's no leak, so this level drop has to be caused by evaporation. This evening we'll hose in water, otherwise the fish will soon be paddling. Not swimming.

Yesterday afternoon, while the spaniel was dozing across the husband's lap, our neighbour knocked on the door. To warn us about foxes. On Saturday afternoon he'd lost eight laying hens and four ducks. He thinks there must have been two predators, working together.

Many years and a house ago, we had two young rescue cats, siblings, who did this. They picked on the weakest baby bunnies in the field adjoining our garden. Sometimes they'd drag a victim in through the kitchen cat-flap – one pulling, one pushing. Clever, efficient and appalling.

The rabbits weren't always dead, or even injured. I vividly remember watching some TV drama one evening, when a young rabbit darted out from behind the screen. Hale and hearty but startled. And hell to catch.

The spaniel was needy at the weekend. No walks, little food, much falling over. He's still drinking and he wags his tail. Much cuddling seems to be necessary. We know that what we're dealing with is a slow goodbye.

Lunch today majored on homemade sourdough baked by my son-in-law. I almost certainly ate too much and am now feeling it. It's warm in the conservatory. The dog whimpered so I lifted him onto the sofa beside me. A fortnight ago I wasn't able to do this alone.

Earth, whisky and water

A month ago, just as we were all remembering VE Day, I was sent a wartime photo by Lisa, a cousin, of her grandfather. Derek was a fabulous man – a people person, fond of children and easy in his manner with everyone. This poem was loosely inspired by him...

Earth and Water

At three a.m. wakefulness can seem a judgement.
In darkness, with owlhoots and wild, nameless
animal cries for company; am back at my uncle's funeral
and before – whisky poured, he turned to ask his wife
of forty-four years what's your poison,

turned back, dropped crumpled to the floor.
The paramedic, a family friend, blubbed plump tears,
said it's a good death, a good way to go,
that he'd be much missed, a glass-half-full bloke,

whose face swims before me, misty, detail
coarsened, then falls back. So on, treading water,
to where I've buried scraps from his funeral. I peel
back the feeling, words said, readings, voices,

Jim Reeves somehow fitting. How they closed
the rainwashed pewter roads in that little town,
chapel filled, they filled the porch, trampled sodden grass
outside to hear his sending off broadcast, crackling out.

They'd come to pay or show respect, the size
of the hole he'd leave, its shape and depth
measurable in that place he'd never left,
would never leave. Had never seen the need.

Full moons, strawberries and a man with a passion

The full moon was last Friday, 5th June. It's known as Rose Moon, Hot Moon or, more commonly, Strawberry Moon. It roughly coincides with the start of the strawberry picking season. Ours, growing inside a polytunnel, are just beginning. I checked on them earlier and only snaffled one. Which was pretty restrained I thought.

July's full moon will be as a Thunder Moon, or Full Buck Moon. But let's not wish the month away. It's furlough payroll time again. Another fortnight has passed. There is a little more freedom, but not much. Wales is closed to visitors. We don't know when business can resume, and in what form. So much we're waiting to find out.

Recently I was sent some information about a distant cousin, whose existence I was totally unaware of. Theodore Ballantyne Blathwayt was born in England but worked in Cape Town and died in Johannesburg in 1934. It was his splendid name which drew me in to read and find out more.

He was the discoverer of three comets – c/1926 B1, C/1927 A1 and a third whose name I haven't been able to establish yet. For each new discovery he was awarded a Donohoe Comet Medal and he was elected as a member of the British Astronomical Society in 1929. I came across articles he'd written where his enthusiasm and individuality was palpable.

He spent many nights 'sweeping' for comets. He writes that he made his finds using a four inch refractor and an eight inch reflecting telescope. I have no idea whether or not this would still be the kit of choice for a modern comet hunter.

Being in a heightened state of readiness, or not

The in-box is full of directions, instructions, imperatives. What happened to 'please' or 'have you considered?' They're all at it – websites, forums, agencies, the bigboy channel managers, the free and not-so-free consultants. Stand out. Get ahead. Catch your competitors napping. Hit the ground running. Make sure you're Covid-ready.

The problem is that it's difficult to prepare for the unknown. More of it. Here, in Wales especially, we don't know what we're going to be allowed to do, how much of it, with what provisos and restrictions, and when. In tourism and the hospitality industry, the future is still very fuzzy. So it's becoming beyond frustrating to be harangued continually. What actions are we taking? What announcements are we going to make on our websites and social media? What reassurances can we give our future guests and customers that we are primed and ready to go?

Apart from anything else, these exhortations to us, as business owners, suggest that there's a huge team of cleaning and maintenance staff here in hazmat suits, raring for the end-of-lockdown whistle to blow. And there isn't. Our little team has been furloughed. We won't be calling anyone in until we have the relevant information from the government, and we can look at it, understand the implications and make a plan. Until then, we're not making guesses or empty promises.

Perhaps I'm not alone in feeling bullied. I've always had rather a glass-half-full role in every situation I've found myself in — a kind of blend of Heidi and Pippi Longstocking. Today, I've let tiredness and grief overwhelm me. But I will be more than ready when it's time.

Grief and a lesson

We've been living here since 2007. The animals we've shared this space with have been, and still are, only pets. We've lost two cats, rescued siblings we brought with us – first Cooper and then Chaplin. Both are buried under the little walnut tree which is not thriving. We've lost two sheep – English Dave, saved from the pot in Buckinghamshire, and the young lamb, Gwilym 1, who died at the hands of a cocky locum vet. A sad waste.

And now both the spaniels. Our two English Springer Spaniels were brothers, bought from the next little farm up the lane in late May 2006. This was the year before we moved here permanently. The surviving one, Dylan, died on Friday, ten weeks and a day after we lost his brother. If he'd had a death certificate I believe 'died of a broken heart' would have been a contributory factor.

In the human world many worse things have happened over the last five or six months. Thousands and thousands have been bereaved and have suffered hugely. Globally it has been a grim year and there is no quick fix to the situation the UK is now in. I get all that, and obviously it is affecting us too.

But this morning we are still in the early stages of processing the loss of our furry companions, the legendary duo, who, for the last fourteen years, played such a key part in the experience of all who lived here or visited.

The lesson I've learnt? Do not acquire two pups from the same litter. The chances are that their lives will come to an end at around the same time. And that is heart-breaking.

Flight and the jynx bird

Finding somewhere which feels like home has a lot to do with luck. This little farm has been our home for thirteen years now, the longest we've lived anywhere. Finding it was a rather odd process, and the 'it' we found wasn't necessarily the 'it' we thought we'd find, or were looking for. In the process of choosing this place, we were shown round some desperately sad smallholdings, where the dreams had soured, the project hadn't worked, the couple had fallen out of love with their home, with rural life and with each other.

But there were good omens on the day we found our home – a hare, and then later, in early evening, dolphins. We were blessed.

The Jynx Bird

In a way I envied the two of you,
the box lid farmyard prettiness, it all
unmarred by serial improvements
ripping it apart.

I saw the pristine canvas, past lives shed.
You arrived, cabin-bags-only, freshly
severed from your partners, your stories
scattered from the Bridge.

You were sold the dream of the new start, bought
your farm, while we turned up trailing baggage,
failing parents, ailing child, itching scabs,
partly mended souls.

We stumbled over tyre mountains, decades
of buried rubble, brambles which burgeoned,

a wealth of unconnected gutters,
mud, flood, persistent rain.

Last five years and you'll stay forever! Like
it was an ordeal or trial. That's what
he said, the deal struck, some hay bought, lobbed
in the back of his truck –

as if weightless. City folk. I prickled.
He shrugged and left. Like we were strange, foolish,
like it was hard. That seen-it-all-before look
in our ramshackle yard.

As if he knew about winter, and the fact
of all we'd had before at the turn of tap,
the flick of switch. We learned to live with
unpredictability...

Yet the Jynx bird picked you, curdled the milk,
turned the hens off laying, drained the well to dust.
In that husk of a home the cracks widened:
you started to hope

for a new chance, another flight. But here,
us, despite all soothsayers, we put down
roots. This place, of all places, has hooked
us in to stay.

Elderflowers – one day at a time

In the afternoon, my daughter popped in to borrow scissors and to check we were ok with her collecting elderflower heads for cordial. There are still plenty left for berries, but higher up, less accessible. We'd saved Welsh apple juice bottles from the bar – months and months ago when the bar was open. I had thoughts of making elderflower liqueur when I woke up yesterday – but listlessness took over.

It was the second morning of waking up in a spaniel-free, dog-free house. Inconsiderate of our need for sleep at night, the cat had brought in one after another mouse to consume at her leisure under the bed. First thing, I'd had to slither underneath to scoop up five piles of small rodent innards. As soon as we'd vacated, post tea and muesli, she fell asleep, replete, on our bed.

For the second consecutive day, Miss Baxter absented herself from the conservatory – on Saturday, probably to avoid a noisy invasion of small people, while two of their parents were making pizzas. Then, on Sunday, her absence was doubtless due to the previous night's strenuous antics and maybe also she was avoiding an embarrassing display of human sentiment. We were looking at spaniel photos and videos on the PC. We hadn't realized there were so many. Lovely memories. But Miss Baxter does not like fuss.

Late afternoon, I tried to pull myself out of the low mood to collect some elderflower heads for my own use. A small bored person appeared, looking for distraction. She helped to strip the flowers from their tiny stalks. Somewhere between two and four weeks from now, we will see how drinkable this liqueur is!

The small person stayed to feed the sheep and help get the stable donkey-ready. She'd tired of the other project on offer in the yard– painting a new house for the growing brood of chicks.

In the evening I felt too exhausted for anything other than submitting to I-player. Our kitchen/living-room felt curiously empty. But it felt good to have done something.

Furlough in the fairy kingdom

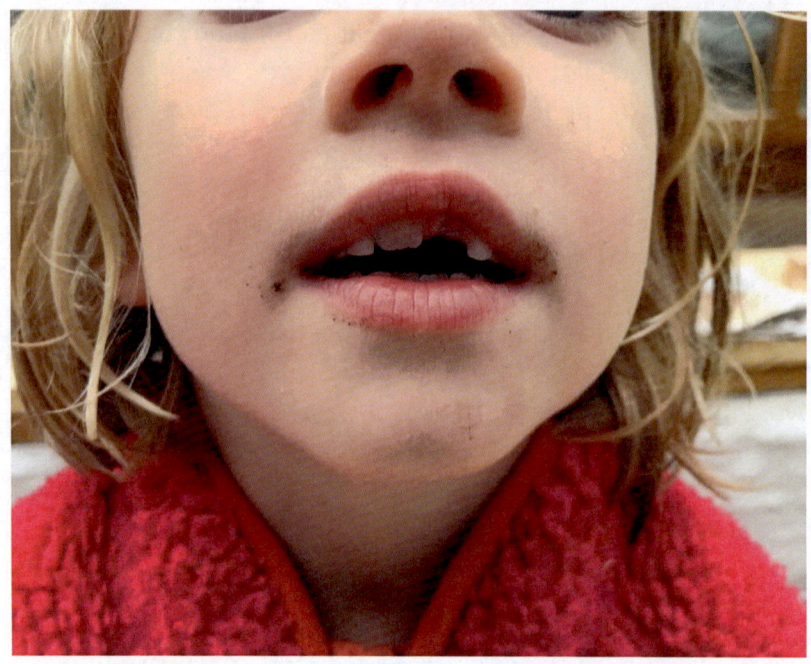

In the three months or so of containment here, there has been much hair, and some teeth, activity. The third little girl now has a neat bob, courtesy of the skills of my daughter-in-law. Despite the Welsh accent, she somehow looks very French.

The guy who lives on the farm with us, (and is helping the husband in the loo block project), has a painful broken tooth. He's waiting for a call-back to discuss when he'll be able to have a socially distanced dental appointment to sort out the problem. The six-year-old with a new haircut has lost two teeth in lockdown. The going rate, I'm told, is £2 for the first one and £1 for each subsequent loss.

I was becoming rather concerned. For three nights the smalls reported that there was a tooth fairy no-show. Was there a late furlough amongst the community of fairy folk? Were they working at reduced capacity and thus taking longer to respond to new under-pillow-packages? Was each sprite overstretched, having to fly over a much wider territory?

Or even, was the lack of entertainment and diversions for children of a wobbly tooth vintage, causing excessive wiggling, a swifter shedding of milk teeth and a greater workload for the already stretched miniature winged creatures? These possibilities and more popped into my head.

Finally, on the fourth night, and without apology, explanation or sicknote, the West Wales designated tooth fairy put in an appearance. Everyday life was visited by magic. All, once more, was well.

Ascot without the crowds

I was asked to write a poem for the opening of this year's Royal Ascot. Poems commissioned for TV are strange hybrids. You write them to a brief. Time, invariably brevity, is of the essence. And it's an odd experience hearing someone else voice your work. Having said all this, it was an honour to be asked again.

This year - Royal Ascot 2020

This year,
east to west, north to south, winds of change
have blown, when all the things we thought we knew
were hurled off kilter, helter-skelter, by gales
of scale we couldn't picture, storms remorseless thwarting,
shifting things we'd worked for, social functions,
sporting fixtures.

This year,
we slipped from roaming where we wanted,
from lack of fear to life lived fearful, home alone. Flung
from old normality into here-and-now, *must-not-hug*;
to judge what matters – oxygen, *lungful gallops,*
hope somehow.

This year,
we've hung rainbows painted for new heroes,
carers, the NHS, selflessness, life-and-death.
Waiting release from house arrest but uplifted
by the Queen's address. *We will meet again.*
Amidst all loss, our clapping's carried
across the ether.

This year,
racegoers, royalty, we'll be at home, sharing
this sporting highlight of British summers, runners and
riders,
this heart-stopping thrill. Three centuries' history,
the best of thoroughbred bests, assembled
for their bravest efforts, amongst great and good
and fashionably dressed.

This year,
we'll tell flat-racing's stories, (Dettori's glories and the
rest),
at TV picnics with bubbly or beer. We'll roar
as we've cheered down the years for Estimate,
brave Frankel, legendary Yeats. Outside these gilded
gates,
we'll make our *virtual turfed reality.*
Celebrate.

This year,
might those strings of Stradivarius be plucked
to perfection again? Let's recall each horse
at full stretch, extended to his limits,
as we have been, our world vibrating
on one shared breath.

The donkeys have a visitor

The farrier has been. We cancelled the last visit because it was too early into lockdown. But, by this week, it had become a necessity. As with sheep shearers, you cannot know an exact arrival time. Even if the farrier is a regular visitor, (so with no chance of getting lost), there are the unknowns about his previous calls. His day had started at 5.30 a.m. and we were fourth on his list.

I was ready early. We'd run out of both carrots and apples but there was no shortage of donkey nuts. The farrier was of course delayed, arriving at 10.15 rather than the estimated 9.30. In anticipation, I had put on both donks' head collars. However, since this is generally a precursor to leading them out, they smelt a rat. Or quite simply realised that something was afoot.

They are, for all their bickering, inseparable. The larger donkey is Top Donk – first to be led in and out of the stable, expecting also that we will approach her first with a head collar and a feed bucket. She is first in the queue for a pedicure also. We have tried to mix it up occasionally, to give the other smaller donk the option of being first. But the natural order is one they are comfortable with. And it always prevails.

Top Donk was just about co-operative with the farrier, compliant provided that a non-stop supply of food was available as bribery. Her companion is less food-driven and far more intelligent. She had plenty of time to view the proceedings and to decide no-thank-you-very-much-and-if-it's-all-the-same-to-you-I'd-rather-not. Second Donk is more than capable of refusing point-blank to fit in with human schedules. If the opportunity had presented itself for her to hoof it, she would have done. One very strong small donkey did have her toenails trimmed eventually but she made her displeasure known.

When the farrier left, the floor of the stable was sprinkled with hoof parings – grubby potato peelings on the outside with a touch of silvery grey iridescence on the inside.

There are limited distractions for children right now, so the whole proceedings were watched in rapt silence by the four smalls. All at a safe distance from the rear end of feisty Second Donk.

Terrible lizards, bluebirds and a painting in the attic

Two of the smalls were around this morning, while their mother snatched a couple of hours' freedom for studying. We were scraping the barrel with the games still unplayed. But Downfall and Connect 4 whiled away a happy hour, while big globs of gloopy, sticky rain landed on the glass above and around us. Despite protests, when a couple of jigsaw puzzles were unearthed, we got stuck in and particularly enjoyed the dinosaur one.

I tried to explain who Dame Vera Lynn was to one of the children. The term 'forces sweetheart' was far too archaic to feature. The small person claimed never to have heard the song

'We'll meet again'. I'm sure it was playing on a loop at our VE Day picnic.

Whatever your position on the political scale, however you regard the Second World War, there was surely something rather splendid – heroic, no-nonsense, lacking in personal vanity – about the dame? Having all your own marbles, being able to hold a tune and reaching 103 is pretty good too. I wondered if people would still be listening to those iconic forties' anthems 50 years from now?

And the Streetcat Bob died a few days ago. Aged 'at least 14'. He must have been, as his transformational relationship with his recovering addict/Big Issue seller human dated from 2007. By all accounts, Bob was a remarkable marmalade feline. I saw the film and blubbed throughout. I might rename our ginger cat 'Vera Roberta' for the weekend.

Miss Baxter brought in a critter while we were having a TV supper and watching Professor Brian Cox on astronomy. The part I saw started with dinosaur footprints. The husband was following the whole thing. I drifted off, deeply impressed by the spareness of the commentary, the flattened yet emotive vowel sounds of the boyman scientist in his black teeshirt and walking trousers. You know the sort of thing.

There may well be a really scary painting in the Professor's attic. There's probably no longer a small mouse under the sofa in the conservatory. It would be good to predict with confidence those mythical bluebirds appearing sometime again soon.

Fathers' Day, a damp squib and an emergency cat

Several of us slept badly on Saturday night – maybe it was the loudness of the rain or the shortness of the night. Several of us felt quite tired and a bit flat on Sunday morning. The paper made for dismal reading. Brains proved inadequate for both crossword and sudokus.

Then, on the way to put the donks out, I rescued a rather beautiful butterfly from one of the barns and we collected a handful of courgettes and small squashes from a polytunnel.

Towards midday, between heavy rain showers, there were visits and presents – three fathers together in the conservatory – the husband, the son-in-law and my elder son. Silverback gorilla, (aka the husband), received chocolate, homemade cards, a painted 'You Rock' stone, a bottle of homemade elderflower cordial and a jar of homemade lime pickle. We drank tea, coffee and squash, sampled the elderflower gift and ate cake. My daughter made a lemon drizzle cake with raspberries. Orla baked cupcakes for the festivities, entirely unaided.

These past three months have been punctuated by small celebrations on the farm – Easter, an anniversary, a birthday, VE Day and then yesterday, Fathers' Day. A whole season has passed. The internet was full of suggestions for make-the-solstice-special-at-home ideas. No-one here was especially inspired. The solstice came and went.

Dependent on the next First Minister bulletin, and of course the 'R' number, it looks like we will be opening guest accommodation from 13th July – a reduced number of yurts, no shared facilities, no camping – but some business. Over the weekend we were updating prices and availability on our website. Plans for the remainder of Summer 2020 are still fluid and we're waiting to receive details about the rules, regulations and protocols. It doesn't quite feel real yet.

Soon we may be able to see other family members and good friends living beyond the current permitted area. That's a definite end-of-tunnel light.

A few of my friends, for various reasons, have been much less fortunate than I have and have spent the last three months more-or-less alone. One has an allotment to keep her busy. One has a beloved small dog. A third is in real need of an emergency cat. We all need something living – if not human company, then something which grows. Or better still, something which breathes and responds to us. I wish I could dispense, where required, an emergency cat or two.

A dragonfly

All four smalls were here yesterday morning; the mother of two of them was doing university work, but the parents of the other two had gone to see a funeral cortege and to watch the funeral remotely through zoom. Deaths are still occurring for other non C-19 reasons. This was a tragic road accident which has left children fatherless. Technology broke down nine minutes into the service.

It felt more like a blustery March day than late June. We all went for a walk before the weather broke – grey clouds were looming. First stop – the horses, who are currently number one attraction for the children. Despite their size, they are much less skittish and unpredictable than the donkeys. And then we walked the fields – a route not taken in nearly two weeks, as the recently deceased spaniel was too frail to walk it in his last few days.

In that fortnight we've had ideal growing conditions for brambles. The only way to get through in places was bearing sticks. The smalls enjoyed this. Creatures abounded – birds, butterflies, ladybirds (that eternally entertaining spot-counting exercise), assorted little bugs and beetles and the most extraordinarily-sized dragonfly, which kept us company for a while. When we googled later, it looked like we'd seen a golden-ringed dragonfly.

Technology here is finally improving after almost a week of at first patchy and then no mobile coverage. Fortunately, we have an office landline and a second internet connection through a different provider, so we weren't totally cut off. But it was extremely frustrating while it lasted. My work computer has yet to be moved back to the farm office from the kitchen table.

There are other concerns, irritations and difficulties right now – a lot to do with communications from government. Announcing changes without having thought through the detail. Basic stuff really. Why should this surprise me?

As often happens, I found myself delving further into dragonfly territory. I started with Tennyson's little poem, (barely clocked before), and then moved on to dragonfly eating habits. A dragonfly has a prodigious appetite, consuming its own weight in insects in 30 minutes. It's carnivorous, and sometimes cannibalistic. Its wings typically beat 30 times per second, compared to an average bee speed of 300 beats per second. Despite lack of speed, the dragonfly is the strongest flyer in the insect world – its strength enabling it to hover even in strong headwinds. A thought to hold onto for a moment.

Lost, lavender and another birthday

George the cat seemed confused. Outside the pizza wagon, on the conservatory windowsill, in the yard, up in the vegetable garden. He's been spending time here for the last few days now, but then, yesterday especially, it was as if he'd forgotten where home was. And he seemed distressed about it.

In the heat of Wednesday and Thursday who could blame him for losing the plot a little? For two days the sheep barely moved till mid-afternoon. A couple of times I had to check that we still had three of them. They were so utterly still. May was, without doubt, a record-breaker, followed by a few weeks of more mixed, more normal Summer days. Then came Wednesday and Thursday. Scorching and humid. Brain foggingly, ankle swellingly humid. The kind of heat when it's impossible to feel fragrant for long.

The barometer is not entirely responsible for my recent sense of being overwhelmed, under-achieved and exhausted. I've found the images of the British beach madness depressing too.

We had thunder and lightning last night; and rain, just enough to clear the air. We watched Bennett's 'Talking Heads' – just the one monologue with the brilliant Sarah Lancashire. Excellently acted but bleak. And Radio 4 was right about the appalling knitwear. Have always found Bennett challenging. He's very talented and has such a great ear for speech, but it's quite a dark, narrow furrow he ploughs.

On what would have been the beginning of the Glasto weekend, it's also my elder son's birthday. Have been round for tea and, inevitably, cake – this time a Hugh F-W carrot cake which my daughter-in-law and two smalls baked bright-and-early this morning. My son took the day off and he woke to smells of baking.

I've never been to Glastonbury, (as in the festival). I love the abbey though. It was the place we visited the day I discovered I was pregnant (with today's birthday boy). I think the scale of the festival would put me off now – smaller festivals, yes, but not something that massive.

The lavender is finally out and spectacular as it always is. I brushed past it earlier. Then, on their way home, the two youngest brought me flowers from the cutting section of one of the polytunnels. And they fed the fish – a pinch each.

A happiness expert spoke on the radio yesterday. 'Happiness,' she said, 'is not having what you want...but wanting what you have.' And, despite all the conflicting emotions, I do.

Chocolate cake and nude trampolining

Miss Baxter climbed on my keyboard yesterday afternoon. I pushed her off and she fell asleep on my mouse mat, nudging the mouse and shedding fine pale hairs with every exhaled breath. I worked around her, relishing her warmth and physical presence inches from my typing fingers. Poor tired puss.

But the amorality and perfidy of cats knocked me sideways again early evening. The boys were still on the roof of the double decker bus, trying to finish the job before rain set in. Hopefully wearing masks and goggles and being careful: the husband has had one or two accidents. I tend to cross digits and look away. I was making an unexciting risotto and chatting on the phone when Miss Baxter came in, dragging something heavy. She darted under a pine cupboard but I'd clocked her.

Half a rabbit. The hind quarters of a rabbit which she'd planned to sneak past me for her delectation later. I was not amused.

Take-out Saturday again, which means looking after two smalls while their mum and dad cook and serve pizzas from lunchtime till mid-evening. This morning, there were flowers to organise to send to the widow of a couple married here not that long ago. Strange and sad that all the optimism, all the joy of that wedding day, had led so quickly to here.

Then there was the socially distanced trip to the village shop-cum-post-office returning stuff, posting cards for an assortment of occasions. But there were three real-time, brief conversations in the queue with neighbours and acquaintances, including one with two dogs which were waiting patiently, tied up outside like trusty steeds outside a western saloon. That sparked the inevitable exchange about the loss of our two. Would we get another dog? It seemed such an odd question.

Delivering post next door before lunch, I was greeted by a trio of little girls bouncing on the trampoline and the three-year-old boy sitting, being bounced.

'We're naked,' they shrieked. They were. 'But it's raining,' I said.

'It's hot rain,' one of them said.

And then the youngest piped up – 'I'm not naked .' And he wasn't.

Activities this afternoon included tracing, drawing, colouring, the sheep and donkey routines, making a chocolate and raspberry cake – mostly orchestrated by the husband, while I acted as chief washer and clearer up to all of them, picking wild cherries, making jam and replying to accommodation enquiries for post July 13th. This is the date tourism unlocking is planned to start in Wales. A friend told me yesterday that there are now twelve empty shops in our little market town, Newcastle Emlyn. The decline has been gradual, but it's accelerated over the last few months. Can it be reversed? I'd like to hope so.

Past Glastonbury highlights on TV are my background music as I write this. It's been a day of cloud and sunshine, wind and rain. Of course, it was hot rain.

Defences breached and fields of flowers

There is a hole in the conservatory. One of the windows broke last night. It's been a mostly grey day today. The temperature has dropped and the chill has been palpable. The timing hasn't been brilliant.

Last time anything like this happened it was three houses back and what feels like a lifetime ago. We were living in, and extending, a modern house. For once, we'd employed a builder. Turned out he was a rogue, who disappeared, leaving his sub-contractors out of pocket and us with a building site, and no windows in the front of the house. The husband was elsewhere, possibly in the Middle East. The weather wasn't good and I had three quite young children. Friends rallied and a posse of other husbands arrived to board up the windows, to protect us from ingress by either weather, uninvited visitors or both. The current problem is minor by comparison and should be fixed tomorrow.

My niece has lost and found a job in the last couple of months. Her first day went well today. The wind was fresh and the donkeys were fast and frisky this morning, relishing their freedom. We played poohsticks on a bridge in the village. With a small, naturally, not with the donkeys.

A friend was talking about how much more closely we look since lockdown, how much more we notice. I've seen this especially with the children and have included an image of a burnet moth, feasting on nectar in our tipi meadow. We're cutting two fields this summer. We have the gear to cut and turn but not to bale, so a local farmer is going to cut and make round bales – either for silage or haylage – from one field. As for the other one, he'll probably cut the grass and take it away in a trailer to be used as cattle bedding.

What we amateurs relish for its prettiness, and for the pleasure it gives to us, is not necessarily a plus for a professional. The farmer picked a bunch of oxeye daisies to take home.

'Cows don't like flowers,' he said.

Art, artists and a competition

The headlines have been proclaiming it's back to school in Wales. This is an over-statement. The eldest small went ba school yesterday morning for three hours. Six children took the invitation to return. They have two more Monday morn in this very different school setting and then, it's the end of term.

In Orla's absence, her younger sister watched the husband working through a small box of things-to-be-fixed. Mostly bits of jewellery. I've always loved jewellery, generally vintage or handmade by a craftsperson. Often with little financial value. But, to my eyes, pretty. Some things were not repairable or ha missing hooks or clasps. My talented sister silversmiths. I know that's a tongue-twister but am not sure if it's a verb. Amazingly, a little package arrived from Buckinghamshire this morning with some spare parts. Thank you, sis!

Years ago, a local painter was running workshops in our Old Dairy. Presumably she had more than enough fish at home as she started populating our little tank-cum-trough, (aka pond 1) with fish. She did this gradually and by stealth. When we had five new aquatic residents, I mentioned this strange occurrence to her. Her face gave her away. Five became four a while back. We've noticed that one of the survivors doesn't seem to be thriving. While we became custodians of goldfish by accident, not design, I don't like to see any creature ail on my watch.

An entry just popped into the letterbox. We've been running an art competition for children here to draw or paint something from the last three months of lockdown. The idea is to use elements from their pictures to create a mural. This would then decorate a rather ugly wall in the farmyard.

The dull, the drab and the dreary has seemed dominant for the last few days. Any bright flower emerging is cause for celebration!

The hole is plugged. Glass now exists where it was formerly absent. It's less draughty. However, when asked if the job was finished, his response was slightly shifty. 'More or less,' he said, 'but don't open the window yet.'

While sweeping up shavings and splinters of wood and other evidence of the recent activity, I came across clouds of soft fine dark hair. This was from Sunday afternoon, a socially distanced visit by a chocolate lab called Millie. Her humans came too.

A postman and two specialists

'It's worse than Christmas,' said the postie. Several building/DIY related parcels arrived for the husband and a gift for me. It was a lovely pack of butterfly playing cards. I predict a heated game of snap very soon.

Today, there was huge excitement. Hot water now comes out of the cute copper taps in the loo block. This hot water is stored in a cylinder which used to live upstairs in the farmhouse (until it sprung tiny leaks). A local guy repaired the tank and it's now being heated up by the second-hand solar panels on the barn roof (first lockdown project). Still a few tweaks necessary, but we're almost there.

Despite changeable weather, the bees are very active. Lavender is popular as ever but there's been a lot of to-and-froing near the last windblown roses on the yard pergola. More by chance than design, these co-exist amiably with jasmine and clematis. Today we have a few new clematis flowers, not a full second flush, but I'm optimistic.

Yesterday a friend passed on good news about her pet's clean bill of health. At its recent annual booster and check-up, her dog's heart was behaving oddly. With great haste, pet and human made their way to a local centre of excellence for doggie tickers. There, every test known to veterinary cardiologists, and pet insurers, was carried out. With hindsight, my friend thinks that her pet's heart irregularities were probably due to panic. Under current C-19 precautions, owner and pet separate at the door of the surgery. The owner waits in the carpark, unable to hold a paw or make encouraging noises...

This tale brought back a time when we too lived in the Home Counties. Rosie, the dog we had, injured her eye badly. Almost immediately, we found ourselves in the consulting rooms of a pet eye specialist. He was a magnificent specimen, with a manner which soothed all canines and their owners, (particularly the female of the species). He also had a helicopter parked jauntily in the clinic garden.

While our patient was convalescing, we went to stay in a farm cottage, one of a pair, near Cardigan. Our next-door neighbours had a black Labrador and, for the three or four days of the mini-break, humans and dogs socialised. One early evening, perhaps over a cup of tea or glass of wine, the couple told us about their recent pet experiences. There was much praise for the vet who had cured their dog. 'And you'd never guess what,' the lady said, 'but on the lawn of the clinic there was a *helicopter*. And it was his.'

Here, we still haven't returned to the halcyon days of accompanying a pet into the vet's surgery. It remains an unnatural and anxious experience

Let them eat cake

So, the five-mile-limit will be dropped from Monday in Wales. Since this started I've only done one trip beyond this limit, to a supermarket in Cardigan. I haven't really felt deprived, except of course, for seeing the family I don't live with, friends beyond the 'zone', the occasional evening out and...the sea. There is a plan to visit the sea one evening, possibly Wednesday, after work.

Confusing opinions abound in the media – many brickbats, some fear, few plaudits. My concern is that the impetus to restart the economy is pushing aside any environmental gains we may have made, amongst the losses of the last few months. I hope we don't just slide back to the way things were.

I also hope that the leaders who have actually done some good, (or even are just wading through this as best they can, but in an honest, compassionate way), are rewarded for their efforts. Not the bamboozlers and the blaggards.

Yesterday, pubs opened in England and it was Independence Day in the US. After seeing some film footage of non-distanced socialising in London, I decided not to depress myself further. I watched one of the Alan Bennett's 'Talking Heads' – this time with Tamsin Greig – reminding myself both of her acting talent and her beautifully expressive eyes. A tour-de-force, but not cheerful viewing either.

It was take-out pizza Saturday yesterday. The son-in-law has been experimenting with gluten-free dough. He's absolutely nailed it now! After responding to some accommodation enquiries – it was, once more, small central here. Activities comprised visiting the horses, feeding the rest of the menagerie, cleaning out and bringing home the donkeys. There was also Hunt the Teddy, a puzzle, a couple of storybooks, watching Jungle Book, (the more recent version), and making, icing and eating cupcakes.

All being well, we'll have our first visitors here from 14th July. So, between now and the two hundred and thirty first anniversary of the Storming of the Bastille, our little smallholding will be a hive of activity. It won't just be the bees. But we'll fuel ourselves with pizza... and cake.

Soundtracks and a guilty secret

Ennio Morricone, conductor, composer and trumpet-player, died yesterday. Amongst a long career of achievements he wrote the scores to over 400 films and TV productions. Westerns were a particularly successful genre for him. Many of his film scores are classics, (including those he wrote for Sergio Leone and Giuseppe Tornatore). They've been absorbed into our popular culture for over 60 years.

The husband is a man of endless resourcefulness, a combination of optimism and problem-solving ability. Recently, I have found myself in a virtual world of ebullient, noisy plumbers. Weekday lunches often have a soundtrack of YouTube tutorials, jolly chaps teaching all sorts of skills not normally on my radar.

We both had one very disturbed night over the weekend. He was fretting over some technical issue and had to get up to draw his way out of the glitch. He then stayed up, wide-awake, to watch a film. Probably involving guns and all things macho. Upstairs, I kept hearing a single plaintive 'mew', one note of anguished cat. It lacked Miss Baxter's range, her ascending scale and volume. The sound occurred every ten minutes or so. I searched the house for an injured animal. Turns out it was a branch, scraping in the wind against a bedroom window, which made those feline-imitating calls of distress.

My current guilty pleasure is wandering through animal rescue websites. I had to stop myself from clicking 'reserve me' next to the image and description of a delinquent, anti-social goat. One bossy sheep, Gwilym, is quite enough.

I wrote a haiku or three yesterday...

Define spaniel?
Committed to living life
with limitless joy.

Your brother could have
had webbed feet. Instead, you ran
joyful – till you stopped.

Just an afterthought.
The cute pup chosen: how could
we leave you behind?

A hard act to follow? For now, I need to keep resisting the lure
of unfriendly goats.

Pizza, fleeces, bees and a tree

I mentioned gluten-free pizza. Finding the perfect flour for a gluten-free pizza dough has taken a long time. But the company we buy our pizza flour from also produces a gluten-free flour. It is, albeit eye-wateringly expensive, amazing.

The youngest and largest sheep, Gwilym, has been getting bossier. When sheep nut treats arrive there's great excitement, followed by a little tussle with Gwyneth. Gwilym wants the lion's share. However, he's usually very respectful of the old lady, Blackberry. Not so today and yesterday. Despite his size and greed, he's more cautious than the girls, less interested in being petted. Though he will now eat from my hand.

We have the beginnings of a plan for their fleeces. I'm not a spinner or knitter, weaver or felter, so insulation is the answer. We're going to wash the fleeces and then incorporate them into the insulation of the upcycled hot water tank for the new showers.

Today, the men worked between and during downpours. It was cats and dogs. Stair rods. When the donkeys finally made it out to their field, I told them to be sensible, take cover in their purpose-built shelter or hide under the trees. I didn't want to find them standing in the rain, at the gate, looking mournful and accusing. Did they listen?

The bus roof repair is completed. Two yurts have been put up and waterproofed. One more to go, as we will only have three bookable this season. We going to have to leave out some of the frills and the non-essentials this year to minimise the risk of infection.

Cleaning materials, PPE and essential pieces of kit arrive almost daily. I'm trying to find the greenest way of complying with all current advice and recommendations. A package which arrived today contained a note saying my order had funded the planting of a tree.

We love trees. Bees too. My daughter, a novice beekeeper, has a surfeit. Her mentor is currently advising her on the setting up of a second hive. There's also a new swarm which arrived a couple of weeks ago and seems to have settled next door. They must like it here. Long may this continue.

One year ago

A friend sent me a picture of the boys making hay a year ago. There was no pandemic, no furlough and there was a sunny window of opportunity between weddings. So we made hay. While the sun shone. Although it looks overcast and brooding in the photo.

Our first guests arrive tomorrow. It's been like a March pre-season flurry of busyness, only it's mid-July. Some of the activity has been the usual stuff – bringing yurts and their contents out of their winter hibernation, putting them up, re-waterproofing them and getting them ready them for occupation. But there have been processes to document, forms to fill in. A lot of paperwork. Added to this has been the return to part-time work of a few of the team, and introducing them to the way things have to be done now. The new normal which is anything but normal. It seems sad that we have to pare down what we provide in accommodation, prune it right back. No frills this season.

There's been productive busyness down the lane. My daughter's hive was overpopulated. Just before the weekend, her beekeeping mentor visited and helped her to set up a second hive.

There are 44 big round wrapped bales waiting to be taken away. This strange year, we decided to sell hay off the field, rather than deal with it ourselves. Three fields were cut and I think they've made haylage.

I'm a romantic. I confess it freely. I love the scent of fresh hay and the look of the small rectangular bales stacked high in a barn. The job has been done anyway. These bales will be gone soon.

Byebye tipi and feeding the sheep

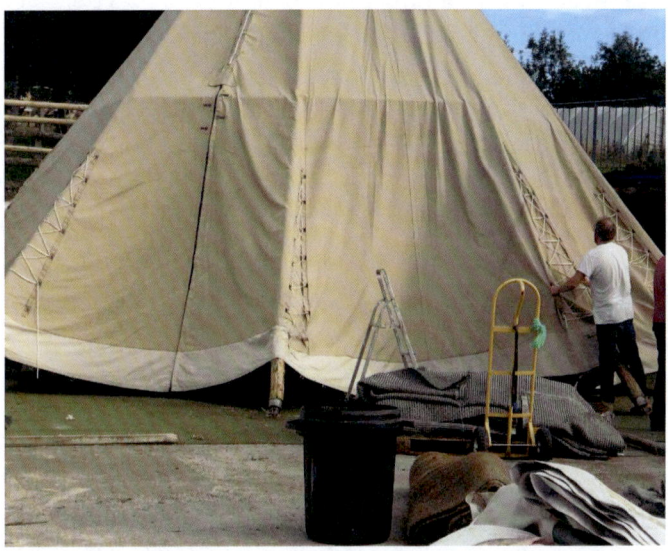

Today the chaps have been taking down one of the tipi frames in the yard. We're going to leave one frame there and cover it – when time permits. But the other canvas is beyond repair. It's over eight years old now so has lasted well!

The frame was made on the farm with Welsh poles we brought back to de-bark here. The canvas was 50% flax and 50% organic canvas. At that time, (the end of 2011 and beginning of 2012), we couldn't find a British giant tipi maker. All giant tipis seemed to be imports. Which is why we chose the self-build route.

Taking down the second skeleton is part of the tidying-up the farmyard project. We plan to offer socially distanced eating and drinking there soon – maybe twice a week. There's painting to do and the creation of a mural based on local children's designs.

However ready you are for guests, it's the last details which eat up time. When you're not on mains – for gas, water or sewage – there's bound to be an occasional glitch too. It's part of the way of life here and keeps us from complacency. But our first visitors have arrived – three units were occupied from yesterday and a fourth today. It's all short breaks. Harder work now though, with the additional hoops to jump through.

The weather has been a bit disappointing for our first two days. Yesterday the forecast worsened as the day moved on. I wanted sun. I wanted our little smallholding to look at its best. But the barometer had other ideas.

The husband, and the guy who lives with us on the farm, have been working long and many days. We've been on a mission to get ready for our partial re-opening. Even the in-theory-office-bound one has been busy physically. According to the gadget on my wrist I walked over 16,000 steps yesterday. No walk, just visitor-preparation activity. For the moment at least, the rather more relaxed way of life of recent months is submerged.

Apparently there was a success on the plumbing front yesterday. It's a complex system here, a black art understood only by the husband. It needs documenting for the 'Clapham omnibus' scenario...though he assures anyone who asks that there are 'schematics'. Would anyone else understand them? I rest my case.

Early yesterday evening I was mucking out the donks and two guests toddled past – a child of about 18 months and his grandfather. I gave them a bucket of sheep treats. Sheep have very soft mouths and nibble gently when hand-fed. It reminds me of one of the really good aspects of doing what we do. And for now, that, and a G&T is enough reward for one evening.

Presence, absence and processing

Life is different, but the 'old normal' shows no sign of returning yet. A steady flow of visitors has been arriving, staying and departing since last Tuesday. 12 days now. We're not currently offering camping, B&B or the big house.

There's more space between bookings. Which is just as well – we are a smaller team and the whole changeover between guests takes longer. There are more processes and safeguards in place. And we're slowly getting used to the new system.

Two of the smalls just asked to feed the fish and we all noticed that the eco pond cleaner has stopped working. Once again, the water is green and gloomy. Also, someone has donated two small yellow plastic bath ducks to the pond. It's a little mystery.

There's been lots of outside activity. A newer yard tipi has been put up. An ugly old farmyard wall is now white. After a couple of weeks of lifting, carrying, climbing and lifting again the husband has hurt his back. Earlier, he took a couple of anti-inflammatory tablets and went for a brief siesta.

While he was resting, a neighbour came to tell me about ragwort – evil poisonous stuff – which has popped up uninvited in one of the fields we use for the donkeys. I immediately went and pulled out what I could. But there was still some left, deep-rooted and resistant to my feeble tugging. Reinforcements arrived in the form of a young male volunteer and the loan of a very conveniently located small fork. The husband emerged just as we'd finished and has now removed all the ragwort we've collected. All's safe in the donkey field for now.

Earlier today I was reading that it's the first anniversary of Mr Johnson as Prime Minister. The headline, I think, was – 'Twelve months at the helm of government.' I'm not sure that's strictly accurate .

Losing things and finding Jane again

Jane Austen is a regular preoccupation. Though not a complete Janiac, quotes and phrases from her novels do pop into my head quite regularly. And soothingly.

It is a truth probably universally acknowledged that a new sock and its mate will soon be parted. I recently received a thank you email from my brother-in-law for a pair of merino walking socks which we sent as a birthday offering. Unexciting, predictable but extremely postable. And he walks a lot, even more so since lockdown. My sister made the sock suggestion and we knew that merino wool would be appreciated. Unlike the husband, my brother-in-law's also the kind of guy who doesn't lose things.

With me, there's a constant loss of pens, not socks. All guests arriving on the farm, whether to stay or to eat, have C-19 contact forms to fill in. Just before a Saturday pizza afternoon/evening,(the first at which guests were going to be able to eat their pizzas outside if they wanted to), the pen shortage had escalated into a mini-crisis. Orla lent me 10 of her store of writing implements, fully believing that she would be able to reclaim them. I'm afraid to say that only 7 remained at the end of the evening.

Early in lockdown I bought three or four packs of pens and stashed them in a top drawer in the farm office. I naively commented to my daughter – 'that'll keep us nicely stocked up for the summer'. All have gone without a trace.

A small delivery of wine arrived about two weeks ago (the first since February). With it came a rather smart pen bearing the logo of the local West Wales wine business. I claimed the pen as mine – not for sharing, not for folks to borrow. Of course it's vanished too.

The last three weeks have been hard, exhausting in fact. Once the donks are in bed, the sheep are fed and we have eaten I have no energy left, especially mental energy. Talking to friends, blogging, reading – all are temporarily on hold. The pendulum has swung too far the other way, but it is as must be for now.

I return to Jane Austen...the other evening, I collapsed happily in front of the concoction that is 'Becoming Jane'. I'd seen it before, probably twice. But it had a watchable cast and sufficient wit to sustain me until bedtime.

Making hay, thunderclaps and uncertainty

It has been a period of incessant activity. Juliet's birthday, Lammastide and another glorious full moon came and went. Barely remarked on.

Weather of all sorts has visited us. Of course there have been blue skies and staggeringly beautiful sunsets. But also days of brain-fogging humidity. Clammy, restless nights. Thunder and lightning. Hot heavy showers. Brief power cuts when the storms were close. For a minute or so technology was extinguished. I was mid-conversation with a prospective guest when this happened two days ago. He rang back. 'I think there's a problem with my phone,' he said. I didn't correct him.

Bad weather is a problem in this holiday business. You feel – or I do anyway – personally responsible – when it rains or is unseasonably cold. Many guests expect perfect, sun-filled days. Some are in lush, green West Wales because their foreign holiday is not feasible or sensible this year. They've been locked in for months and their more exotic plans are just not going to happen this summer. And some visitors are here because they know us, have been here before and understand the vagaries of the UK climate.

I am aware of the emotional investment in a short break to the Welsh countryside. I want, in some small way, for a stay on our little farm to replenish these visitors after months of confinement. And I want them to appreciate what an amazing part of the UK we live in... Most do, I think.

Making long-term plans is impossible now. But today we're making hay instead, with thunderclaps in the distance and the odd scary shower. This hay will feed our pampered pets for the winter. We have no illusions at all about being 'real' farmers.

It was stickiness in the extreme earlier. Even Miss Baxter looked worn out, overwhelmed by the heat, albeit in a languid feline kind of way. Two buzzards and a red kite circled above the farmyard this afternoon. The newly turned grass was obviously the draw, but, to us, it seemed as if they were waiting for one of us to drop.

Hay is being baled, despite late afternoon thunderclaps and fat globules of rain. The husband rang down earlier. 'Get help,' he said. 'There's more than we thought.'

Supper will be late tonight.

Fall falls early, barn camping and the inspection of feet.

And now it's September. We have been seizing the day or making the most of a flurry of staycation activity. A whole month has gone by. My blue notebook is filled with scribbles – such a long time since my writing was neat or even legible – but they've not made it to the blog. So I must apologise for my tardiness and try to catch up with extracts from my notes!

'Almost the bank holiday. Almost the end of August. And, buffeted by the latest storm – Francis I think – it feels like Autumn is here already. Branches are laden, still very green but now weighed down by fruit and ripening nuts. The loss of a bough in high summer wind is a much more serious proposition than it would be in November or February. We drove up the lane earlier to get animal feed – donkey nuts were still unavailable due to a problem with deliveries – and there were sticks, twigs and small branches everywhere, several getting caught under the car.'

Keats was so right! I do love Autumn – mist in the mornings, cooler evenings, scents of ripeness on the air and underfoot. Crispness to come. But we did not welcome that blustery intruder in late August.

Warmth, humidity and wetness didn't do any favours for two of the outdoor pets – one sheep and one donkey. There were weeks of checking feet and applying, amidst strong protests, the purple spray. Of the two donkeys, Treacle seems susceptible to anything going – infections, allergies, thrush... Now both of them have begun to look scruffy again, losing their glossy summer coats and acquiring the unkempt between-seasons look.

As ever, I was concerned about our guests, sharing their disappointment about 'unseasonal' weather. In the midst of the worst rain two families of campers abandoned ship, or rather canvas, and slept on the floor of the barn.

Unlocking seemed to be progressing everywhere with news of new cases, new 'spikes' outside the UK being consigned to the footnotes of journalism. We read articles with graphs showing, beyond the possibility of contradiction, that cases of C19 were climbing again.

'It's our fault, our own stupidity,' one of the barn campers said as he left. *'We are the virus'*.

A scintilla of hope; a whisper of sadness

Another year. It's January 7th . It's been nearly four months since I last posted. Hope, expectation, disappointment, worry, frustration. Repeat. Repeat again. It seems we can cope with confinement, with a barrage of financial, personal and professional body-blows, with travelling blindfolded through a long, dismal tunnel, but coping strategies have now worn very thin. We do need to feed our capacity for optimism.

And we're not all singing from the same hymn sheet any more. We're negotiating the same choppy, troubled waters but in different ways and in different crafts. With less tolerance than before. Like many others, I'm pinning my fragile new 2021 shoots of hope on the vaccine rollout.

Now that the festive season has been and gone, (more 'no' than 'ho' this year), new novels and the jigsaw puzzle have given way to screen dependence again. Generally underwhelming, with no binge-worthy offerings based around chess or the monarchy. However, I did expect good things from the second series of 'Staged', (with Michael Sheen and David Tennant). None of those good things was forthcoming. And who would have thought that the word 'f***' would pop up quite so many times in one 15 minute episode – I stopped counting at 30 – or that the word 'scintilla' would be uttered twice (in the same episode)?

2020 ended with rare snowfall. Only a couple of centimetres, but it's been icy, frosty and bitterly cold for a week. Today, the last remnants of polar frosty stuff gather in corners and cling to rooves. The donkeys stayed in as their paddock was crisp and white.

And the vet visited this afternoon. Blackberry, our eldest pet sheep, had reached the end. We'd been waiting for her to slip away since before Christmas. She clung on – arthritic, wavering on her pins, getting thinner, falling over and needing to be set upright again. Every morning she still greeted us, the tamest and most vocal sheep of my recent acquaintance. *Just a sheep?* Tonight, there's a feeling of relief and inevitability with a little tinge of sadness.

Thaw and a theft

It's slightly warmer today, but there are still treacherous icy patches. Water to all the outside taps is frozen. It's just after five and feels like hunkering down time! Were it not for dry January, some homemade sloe gin would have my name on it right now. The outside animals – donkeys and our remaining two sheep – have been checked on; we've done the afternoon dog walk. It's dark and I've just shut out the outside world by drawing curtains.

I've been nursing the woodburner into life but she's currently uncooperative. Today, she's a luxury, a nice-to-have evening extra. We had two days – two very cold days – with no woodchip, so no central heating or hot water. My son has now part-filled the hopper by tractor so the biomass boiler is fuelled and running once more.

The frost had thawed enough by lunchtime today for us to take the donkeys over to their usual field for a kick about. Since the

New Year they've had a couple of days in just mooching and eating hay, and a couple of days of us popping them into the old sheep paddock for a couple of hours in the afternoons. Weather has certainly altered their routine over the last week. Except for the farrier, who made it to us mid-week for the seven-weekly pedicure. A rare but essential visitor.

Yesterday I baked – banana bread and an orange cake. I forget how far the new dog can reach when standing on hind legs. I forget how observant, how bright she is. In a five minute absence from the kitchen she hooked a slender front paw onto and through the cooling tray and helped herself to a third of the orange cake. No adverse effects this morning though.

We've had her for four months. Her outright terror has diminished but she still barks at people, is wary generally of humans. Dogs she loves. Walks she loves. When we're out with her she's less nervous if she sees a stranger with a dog. Whatever happened to her before we brought her home from the rescue centre has scarred her.

To us she's affectionate and responsive...but we still have a long, long way to go and the outcome, (as are all outcomes now), is unknown and unknowable.

A birthday. The temporary trimming of wings.

Five degrees today. The frost and ice have gone. As have blue skies. It's been grey and damp, a light mizzle in the air. And now stillness has been replaced by wind moaning as it circles the farmhouse.

It's my nephew's birthday. Twenty four today. Because of the lockdown he's not out celebrating with friends in Bristol. He's not doing the real-time activities he loves. He's at home with his parents in rural Buckinghamshire. We've just sung 'Happy Birthday', waved sparklers and watched him eat chocolate cake – virtually.

It was a snowy January night when I drove to my sister's house to babysit his sister, so that his parents could go to the local hospital for his birth. There is a poem, (of course), about that drive and that night, but that's for another day! For now, here's another piece, a short poem inspired by the focus and determination of my nephew – Huw (for himself), William (for his grandfather).

Boy, playing.

At lunchtime, sausages untouched,
neither sitting nor standing, but
quivering on jack-knifed leg; front teeth,
quite new, clamped tight over lower lip,
(frowning like his granddad, his uncle,
before a penalty is taken),
faint humming stirs a straight light fringe.

And that small device, which beeps, has lights,
cannot be prised from nimble fingers
for a wash, for food or drink, for aught
except a clap of exultation,
brief table drumming of his success –

as with those skittering, deft digits,
he scales the heights, his best score yet.

Huw was always going places. Of course no-one is going anywhere this January. But horizons will extend, and freedom, fun and frolics will return one day soon.

The first daffodil

The first daffodils. One is flowering and one is almost. It seems incongruous, as the snow has only gone in the last couple of days. Green bulb shoots are evident everywhere, popping up through mulched brown leaves and grass, but not a suggestion yet of a crocus or a snowdrop appearing.

And I posted a card – to the parents of a New Year's Day new baby boy. My daughter-in-law has just come round to borrow my fairy cake tin for a home schooling maths lesson. My nephew has challenged the husband to Zoom chess at the weekend.

It's getting dark and Jenny's now curled up in her basket by the radiator. We all got muddy on our walk this afternoon and, once again I proved to myself, as I squelched and slid through mud and leaves, that I'm no mountain goat. Unlike the Capricornian husband.

Post festive season viewing is very lean. We watched 'Traces' – ok but nothing special, gave up on 'The Great', about Catherine the Great, after two episodes – (disappointingly daft), and whiled away an hour or two with Tom Hanks in 'Cast Away'. Somehow I missed that one the first time round. Mildly diverting but forgettable were the biopic 'I am Woman' about the life of Helen Reddy, about whom I knew absolutely zilch, and a silly 2010 crime caper with a good cast, including Bill Nighy and Emily Blunt – 'Wild Target'.

What was more interesting than the two latter films was the google and Wikipedia fun afterwards, finding out more about Helen Reddy, and trawling through all the famous, and infamous, Blunts. Twenty years ago, a couple would have watched a film and all the 'I wonders' and 'wasn't that the guy who was in…' would have remained just that. A few minutes of curiosity and random speculation with no probable satisfactory solution.

It's the time of day when what-do-you-want-to-eat discussions happen and when I dread the turning on of TV or radio to hear the evening news – with the three constants – the pandemic/vaccine rollout/latest horrendous statistics, the next chapter in the unbelievable presidency election and election aftermath and the post-Brexit delays, glitches and hiccoughs. I dread it all but find it compulsive.

A laidback mouse, and soulfood

"An artist is an ordinary person who can take ordinary things and make them special." I came across this quote today.

Last Christmas my daughter bought several of her presents through 'Not on Amazon'. We were all trying to buck the ubiquitousness of the big A. One gift was a bottle of Gangplank Cordials' ginger and lime variety, (made in small batches by foraging folk who live on a narrowboat). Delicious, but all gone.

I caught a few minutes of Radio 4's 'Open Book' this afternoon, (between stocking up with donkey and cat food and walking Jenny). The talk was about a children's book – 'Frederick' by Leo Lionni . The eponymous hero is a non-team player field mouse. Frederick refuses to join the other small rodents in stockpiling wheat, corn, nuts and straw for the winter. He spends his summer daydreaming, idling about, apparently not contributing to the greater good of the mouse community.

Frederick defends his apparent inactivity – saying that he, instead, is garnering the suns' rays, the colours of flowers and plants... and words. His rationale? What he's gathering will sustain the mice through the cold, drab and long winter days. And of course, that's what happens.

On my return I downloaded the book – a deceptively simple apologia for non-material values, and for the importance of spiritual and cultural nourishment. Eric Carle, (yes the caterpillar chap), wrote that Frederick 'is a poet from the tip of his nose to the end of his tail' demonstrating 'that a seemingly purposeless life is far from that.'

A friend told me that she needs a project now – painting or sewing or knitting. She needs to be creating something. The lockdown poetry anthology I have a poem in will be published this Spring. Writing poetry has ebbed and flowed in recent years, more ebbing than flowing if I'm honest. But a switch has been turned. Writing is once more an absolute necessity for me.

Healing, holiness and history

Lichfield Cathedral is the first UK cathedral to be used as a Coronavirus vaccination centre. And why not? It's a huge undercover space, and, quite probably, it's underutilised. It seems fitting for cathedrals to be places of healing once more, and for the community to benefit from their existence.

The second daff is flowering. Days slowly lengthen. I started walking at 4.20 yesterday and was still back, after a fairly brisk circuit of the fields with Jennydog, before darkness fell. She's been unwell for the last couple of days – probably to do with eating something disgusting – so I've taken her off her normal food and put her on bland stuff (including boiled rice). She's much improved.

Despite being closed to visitors, this little farm still needs to be looked after and maintained. Things wear out. Things break. Yesterday the chaps, (the husband plus one other), were remaking and repairing a short run of wooden fencing. They just finished before the light went.

They're at it again – my sister and my cousin – on the family tree/history trail. Regular updates are popping in by text, message and email. My sister's tracing the Mansells back, (the direct line from our father), to South rather than West Wales. It's quite a task as more ordinary folk tend to leave less of a written trail.

My cousin sends more random nuggets of information, often about the Blathwayts (from my father's mother's line). Friday's snippet was that we share a seventh cousin – Benedict Blathwayt, a children's writer. Without visual aids, I'm afraid a seventh cousin is a connection too far for me to grasp.

The smalls next door in the cottage were drawing and painting yesterday – a competition entry for Santes Dwynwen's Day on 25th January. Though nowhere near as ubiquitous as Valentine's Day celebrations, poor Dwynwen, (unhappy in love according to the tales), is widely commemorated in Wales now as the patron saint of lovers. She's also known as the patron saint of sick animals.

Insomnia, a delinquent cat and a bear named Pooh

And in that warm cocoon, I am up against the faceless man once more. I've had my second guess at today's five words and not guessed right. So back I go to the locked room until tomorrow, frustrated with failure and at the unfairness of it all. It should be a place of sanctuary but I'm restless, sleeping fitfully and dreaming endless, unsettling dreams.

Over the last month or two I've been flexing the writing muscles with a weekly five word challenge – five words, once a week, from which I must create a poem. The last of these challenges starts today. It's something I thought I was enjoying but, at night, the mind behaves oddly!

Yesterday was Blue Monday – supposedly the bleakest, darkest day. Something to do with lack of sunlight, the dip after Yule and Hogmanay festivities, (not a huge number of these this year), feeling disheartened at the breaking of New Year's resolutions and so on. The weather performed accordingly. Not cold but wet and grey, grey, grey with promises of worse to come – Storm Christoph.

Miss Baxter, our adopted stray ginger moggy, has reverted to her formal feral manners. She's inviting in, or not shooing out, the neighbouring neutered tom. The conservatory reeks of unpleasant feline aromas this morning. Miss B is also having a few 'accidents'…maybe because the outside is less appealing at this time of year. Not expending her considerable energy in the great outdoors means she has a surplus when inside. Midnight craziness is what happens when she's in our room. And when she's not, because we've closed the door, loud vocal objections and destruction of the landing carpet edges are our reward.

Yesterday was also A.A. Milne's birthday. He was born in 1882. As a child I first loved both E.H. Shepard's illustrations and the poems. I still more-or-less know a few by heart, including 'The King's Breakfast', 'Says Alice' and 'Disobedience'. But it's the characters Milne created, Pooh, his friend Piglet and all other inhabitants of the Hundred Acre Wood, who still resonate with children, of all ages, including me. Expunge Disney from your memory. Open Winnie the Pooh at random and something small, simply expressed and perfect will jump off the page and grip your heart tightly.

Unless of course you're obsessed with the spelling of Tuesday, or, like Rabbit, you are clever and have Brain..."I suppose," said Pooh, "that's why he never understands anything."

A lot of water, and another birthday

The smallest small turns four. It's been a dinosaury kind of day – dino cake, dino-themed cards and presents. Yesterday he and his sister helped my daughter make both the cake and dinosaur-shaped biscuits in readiness for today's birthday tea.

The weather has been truly dreadful. It seems like everywhere is either damp, waterlogged or leaking, but at least we're not afflicted by flooding here at the farm. There are many folk in other parts of the UK, and not so far away either, who are badly affected. My son had a complicated trip home from work in Pembrokeshire today due to roads being blocked by water. Storm Christoph is to blame.

But back to birthday boy. I wrote a little poem this morning, inspired by his fascination with those terrible lizards.

The pull of the lizards

Seen on cartoons, in books, as toys – he knows them all.
Herbivore,
carnivore,
omnivore;
voracious in their appetites; he can say their names,
their terrain of choice, their habits, likes. Their world
fills his games.

This little boy, like many more, he knows them all.
Real creatures stalk his world. They populate
his days, his nights. He likes them mean
and likes them nice. He likes them huge
with an enormous roar. It doesn't matter
that they're extinct, that they're not here now.
He knows they lived and thrived before.

He likes them good but the bad, somehow,
are better, more exciting. He knows their names.
The terrible lizards' pull survives; they fill
the minds of most small boys.

In the games he plays on the kitchen floor, he likes
them huge with a very loud roar. It's safer now
they're not here anymore; those terrible lizards –
who lived and thrived and were fierce once before.
He knows their names-
all the dinosaurs.

March and here we are again.

It was my birthday yesterday. March 12th. My sister sent flowers, as did an old schoolfriend. My son delivered a mauve-pink hellebore in a pot – a Lenten rose. In the morning, there were freshly picked daffodils on the table at breakfast. I've been feeling as spoilt as it's possible to feel in these odd times.

The last time I stayed away from home was for just one night, the night of March 11th, in a hotel near Haverfordwest. A few things jump out from my memories of that jaunt – driving with Radio 4 on, listening to the Budget. Marvelling at the Chancellor's total focus on trying to minimise the effects of the pandemic on the economy and on business. To be honest, we weren't yet taking the situation seriously. We hadn't grasped the impact the pandemic would have on our lives. We were still optimistic, still naïve. The hotel stay was unremarkable. We didn't eat there that evening as there was little to tempt our non-standard diets. Instead we drove to the Pembrokeshire coast, to a chilly, blustery Little Haven where we ate in a friendly pub. Afterwards, there was a charity quiz in which we came last. A total disgrace.

On the morning of that last birthday, we wandered briefly around the overgrown part of the grounds, where we learned that Sir William Hamilton was buried next to his first wife, Caroline. His second wife became, of course, Nelson's mistress, Emma Hamilton. There was a leisurely trip back talking mostly about the predicted lockdown.

It would be four days till the announcement about stopping 'unnecessary travel'. Then, of course Boris, pulled the plug on that much abused word, 'normality', on March 23rd. A whole year. Now there's a 'roadmap' out of all this. Whatever happened to that perfectly useful word – PLAN? Tourism will be starting up again in a couple of weeks. Slowly at first, with all the usual restrictions and caveats. I'm cautiously positive. But my priorities have changed. I'm ready to step back from being consumed by this family enterprise.

It's taken a succession of lockdowns for me to realise that writing is what I want to concentrate on now. I started writing more poems again last Spring, then began this little blog. Recently, I've finished a children's book, about mice! I'm hoping to get it published. We'll see...

So, it's been an unimaginably confined and confused year for all of us certainly, but a year where I've rediscovered some of what's important to me. Now, I just need to make it happen!

Afterwards.

The mouse book was published. The publishers ceased trading. I went from elation to despair to creative limbo again. The smalls have grown as children do; the youngest will be six in January. Dodie, a second canine, joined the anxious rescued collie, Jenny. Our world is spanieled once more. There was a house move, just a few yards away. Followed by an accident – there were donkeys involved and I did not come out of it well - and then Covid in January 2022.

In the aftermath of C19, I developed asthma and the tiredness lingered. But poems are being written again, as is a first memoir. There have been a few small successes. For me, and for all the humans and animals I care about, I am crossing all available digits for 2023!

About the author:

Simone Mansell Broome is Welsh-born. She studied English with American Studies at Sussex University, qualified both as a teacher of Speech and Drama and of EFL and taught privately, and at secondary and further education levels. There was a period of fifteen years or so working alongside her husband in two successful small businesses. After being a very long time on the other side of the Severn Bridge, she returned to Wales in 2007 to live and work on a small organic farm.

This farm has grown into a thriving family business with sustainability and community values at its core: it operates as a centre for 'alternative' weddings, for holidays – especially glamping holidays, for a variety of workshops and courses and as a 'pop-up restaurant'.

Simone has been recorded on Poetcasting and her poems have been read on radio and TV. Simone is a member of Second Light network of women poets & has poems on the 'poetrypf' website.

Fifty of Simone's poems were translated into Romanian in 2020 as part of a Bucharest University M.A. dissertation. Simone has been commissioned to write poems by ITV, by a local theatre group and an art gallery.

Simone's first children's book, about a family of mice living through lockdown, was published by Pretty Pug publishing in June 2021 - **'Valletta and the Year of Changes'** . Simone is currently working on a memoir.

Discover other titles by Simone Mansell Broome

Not Exactly Getting Anywhere But - Poems

Juice of the Lemon - Poems

Cardiff Bay Lunch - Poems

Valletta and the Year of Changes – Children's fiction

Included in many magazines, ezines and poetry and prose anthologies. The most recent anthologies containing one of Simone's poems have been

Poems for the Year 2020 (Shoestring Press, 2021)

Gwrthyfel/Uprising, an anthology of radical poetry from contemporary Wales (Culture Matters, 2022)

 simonemb

 Simone@SimoneMansellBroome.com

 broomesimone

 www.SimoneMansellBroome.com

 simonemansellbroome